Prosecution Stories

Prosecution Stories

by
Bennett L. Gershman

Twelve Tables Press
XII

www.twelvetablespress.com

P.O. Box 568
Northport, New York 11768

Library of Congress Cataloging-in-Publication Data

Name: Bennett L. Gershman
Title: Prosecution Stories
Description: Northport, New York: Twelve Tables Press, 2017
ISBN: 978-1-946074-10-2
Subjects: Law—United States/Criminal Law,
LC record available at https:lccn.loc.gov/

Twelve Tables Press, LLC
P.O. Box 568
Northport, New York 11768
Telephone (631) 241-1148
Fax: (631) 754-1913
www.twelvetablespress.com

Printed in the United States of America

To Becky, Benji, David, and Jack.

Table of Contents

Acknowledgments

This book probably would never have been written without the help, inspiration, and friendship of many persons. Mel Glass, the complaints bureau chief, taught us how to be good prosecutors and good persons. Michael Juviler, my appeals bureau chief, taught me how to think clearly, write well, and do justice. Larry Goldman, my colleague then and friend now, inspired me to focus on the use and misuse of prosecutorial power. Joel Cohen, a frequent collaborator who worked alongside me in the special prosecutor's office, taught me how to be a responsible critic of prosecutorial power. Vicky Gannon, my longtime research assistant, kept me alert to news, changes, and trends in prosecution. Ellen Yaroshefsky has been a mentor and courageous voice for ethics reform. Anything I write would not be written without the support, companionship, inspiration, and love of a remarkable teacher, scholar, and moral force in my life, my wife Lissa.

I am grateful to the many others who have educated and inspired me, especially Bill Bastuk, Adele Bernhard, Tucker Carrington, Michael Cassidy, Jeffrey Deskovic, Bruce Green, Tom Hoffman, Peter Joy, Herman Kaufman, Sam Levine, Laurie Levenson, Kevin McMunigle, Dan Medwed, Vanessa

Merton, Tom McDonnell, Marie Newman, Ellen Podgor, Kathleen Ridolfi, Marvin Schechter, and Abbe Smith. These people continue to set a standard of intelligence, integrity, and service that gives me hope that the criminal justice system can be fair, compassionate, and effective.

I would also like to thank Hannah Estreicher for making the manuscript more readable and Sharon Ray for the cover design.

Introduction

Why Tell These Stories?

When I was a young boy of no more than seven or eight years old, I used to listen to the radio as I went to bed at night. One program always stood out. It was called "Mr. District Attorney." I remember the opening lines vividly: "Mr. District Attorney! Champion of the People! Guardian of Our Fundamental Rights to Life, Liberty, and the Pursuit of Happiness." The show featured dramatic stories of prosecutors and prosecutions.

This book is also an attempt to tell stories about prosecutors and prosecutions. I was a prosecutor for many years but this book is not a memoir, although I am part of some of the stories; this book is not a compilation of famous criminal cases, although some of the cases will be recognizable. This book doesn't try to glamorize or demonize prosecutors; the cases, anecdotes, and experiences speak for themselves. This book shows emphatically that the prosecutor is the most powerful official in American government. The book is an attempt to help students, new lawyers, and others interested in criminal law understand how the prosecutor uses, and misuses, this extraordinary power to convict wrongdoers and vindicate the criminal law, while at the same time subject to an array of legal and ethical constraints on the exercise of that power. Also, what happens when prosecutors misuse their power?

There are roughly 50,000 federal, state, and local prosecutors nationwide. This book describes how these prosecutors are featured in criminal courtrooms in America as the producer, director, and star of a system that processes thousands of criminal cases a week. As we shall see, virtually every important decision in a criminal case is made by the prosecutor: who to investigate, who to charge, what to charge, who to reward, who to punish, and how much to punish. These decisions are momentous. While they help protect citizens and provide the safety of communities, these decisions also destroy people's lives, break up families, ruin reputations, and imprison people with more substantial punishments than any other country in the world. And most strikingly, prosecutors wield their enormous powers without any meaningful supervision or accountability.

The use and misuse of prosecutorial power often make headlines. On the dark side, prosecutors like Andrew Thomas, district attorney of Phoenix, Arizona, along with his sidekick, the infamous Sheriff Joe Arpaio, engaged in a ruthless five-year reign of terror against judges, municipal leaders, and lawyers. The office of Charles Hynes, district attorney in Brooklyn, New York, was responsible for a record number of wrongful convictions. A team of elite federal prosecutors deliberately hid exculpatory evidence to bring down the late U.S. senator Ted Stevens. North Carolina prosecutor Michael Nifong, in order to win a tough election, brought unsubstantiated rape charges against three Duke Lacrosse players who were innocent of wrongdoing.

But on the bright side, there are many outstanding prosecutors like Craig Watkins in Dallas, Texas, Kym Worthy in Wayne County, Michigan, Jeffrey Rosen in Santa Clara, California, and the late Ken Thompson in Brooklyn, New York, who have created Conviction Integrity Units to review claims of wrongful convictions by their office and have generally spearheaded innovative law enforcement programs to protect the community and serve justice.

Indeed, the prosecutor has been explicitly called a "Minister of Justice." The prosecutor is legally and ethically mandated not just to win convictions but to seek justice. Most prosecutors try to do the right thing. For these prosecutors, convicting guilty people is important, but equally important is freeing innocent people. The prosecutor has rightly been called a "Champion of the People" who is committed to making the community safe in a battle against lawbreakers. For most prosecutors, not everyone arrested is a lawbreaker. Some prosecutors believe, understandably, that most persons accused of a crime are probably guilty. But most prosecutors see themselves not as zealots seeking punishment of lawbreakers, but as neutral officials with a mission to administer justice fairly and impartially.

Prosecutors are admonished to play fair, in the words of the U.S. Supreme Court to "strike hard blows," but not "foul blows." Foul blows happen. Federal judge Alex Kozinski recently described prosecutorial misconduct as an "epidemic." Experts in cognitive psychology who have studied the prosecutor's conduct recognize that various cognitive biases may impact on a prosecutor's conduct that can lead to overestimating the strength of a case ("confirmation bias"), make it difficult for a prosecutor to maintain an open mind ("tunnel vision"), and cause the prosecutor to discount evidence of innocence ("selective information processing" and "belief perseverance").

This book is about the "hard strikes" as well as "foul blows" that prosecutors commit. As a former prosecutor, academic, defense lawyer, and expert witness, I've watched for a long time how prosecutors behave. To me, it is indisputable that a prosecutor confronts the most daunting challenge of any government official. A prosecutor has the lawful power to take away a person's liberty, reputation, and even life itself. Prosecutors are admonished by legal rules, ethical standards, court opinions, and office manuals not to cross the legal and ethical line of proper conduct, but these guideposts are broadly and often vaguely defined. Given these abstract markers, it may often be difficult for a responsible prosecutor to locate exactly where that line is situated. And even when the line may be clearly delineated, one of the most enormous challenges for any good prosecutor is to get close to the line without crossing it. A prosecutor often has to walk a tightrope in protecting society's interests aggressively against an equally aggressive defense attorney, while at the same time trying to serve justice.

This book also shows how the prosecutor's power has been systematically augmented by courts and lawmakers. Prosecutors have been armed with an increasing arsenal of new legal weapons to fight crime. A vast array of criminal statutes give prosecutors powerful ammunition to fight terrorism, corruption, racketeering, drugs, and financial fraud more aggressively, and give prosecutors much more leverage to punish offenders through enhanced punishments and charges carrying mandatory minimum sentences. Indeed, the possibility of sentences ranging from twenty years to life for a minor drug offense upon an offender with a modest criminal record has given prosecutors the ability to compel cooperation and guilty pleas, even from persons who may be innocent. Critics claim that the U.S. criminal justice system has reached a point where we imprison more people for longer periods of time than any other country in the world. It is the prosecutor who bears significant responsibility for this condition.

This book has two major themes. Firstly, it explains why—for good or ill—the prosecutor is the most powerful figure in the criminal justice system. Secondly, it explains how prosecutors use their prodigious power not only to serve justice, but also to produce alarming injustices. An objective of this book is long range reform. It is worth considering whether current restraints on some prosecutorial excesses are effective. Educating the public about the difficulty of a prosecutor trying to serve justice while getting convictions—as this book tries to do—may help bring about reform.

These stories are all memorable in different ways. They represent a significant part of my postgraduate legal education. They remind me of what it felt like to be a young prosecutor just starting out in an office described by a journalist as a "Ministry of Justice." The ethos in that office was quite remarkable and should inspire a culture of justice in every prosecutor's office in the country.

These stories illuminate the many roles that prosecutors play, well beyond the familiar charging, plea bargaining, and litigation functions. These stories do not necessarily reveal anything unique about what a prosecutor's role is or should be. I am sure that people reading this book will come away with very different impressions and opinions about prosecutors. Suffice to say it that stories of significant events in the work of prosecutors may be meaningful in imagining or reimagining what an ideal prosecutor should be like. It is indeed a challenge to imagine how prosecutors should conceive of their work in order for them to play the most salutary role in our society. This challenge should not be just for those who are prosecutors but for those who have never served as prosecutors but aspire to become prosecutors. In the end, my hope is that these stories may contribute to a better understanding of the prosecutor as a special guardian of justice.

Chapter One

Prosecutorial Discretion

Background

The prosecutor's decision to institute criminal charges is the broadest and least regulated power in American criminal law. Prosecutors are presumed to act in good faith when bringing charges and the courts, lacking knowledge and expertise in law enforcement priorities, almost always defer to the prosecutor's choices. There are no significant constitutional or statutory constraints on charging. Judicial noninterference is reinforced by the doctrine of Separation of Powers, which typically insulates the Executive Branch from extensive judicial review. If sufficient evidence exists, and no improper motivation is shown, the prosecutor's charging decision is virtually immune from legal attack.

This is not to say that the prosecutor's discretion is unlimited. Various legal, political, experiential, and ethical considerations inform and guide the charging decision. But still, there is no subject in criminal law that is as complex and elusive as that of prosecutorial discretion in the charging process. Perhaps the most intractable problem in criminal law is ensuring responsible decision-making by the most powerful official who is authorized to make complex and controversial evaluations of harm, proof, and culpability in a system that allows that official virtually unfettered power to make the most momentous choices that can destroy a person's reputation, liberty, and even life itself.

The following stories are true. They present realistic, recurring, and controversial challenges to the prosecutor's charging power. They involve difficult choices, a tension between moral accountability and mercy, and how a sense of justice can be seen as justification for the prosecutor's decision to do whatever the prosecutor believes is the most just result.

Resolving Tough Choices

Date Rape, the Story of Jane

Prosecutors in making charging decisions often must evaluate the truthfulness of the victim. The following rape case presents the question starkly. Jane went to the police station on a Monday morning with the following account. She told the police that on the previous Saturday evening, she had a date with Ed and that she had never dated Ed before. Jane was twenty-eight and unmarried. She has been an associate in a large law firm for several years. She first met Ed, an attorney in another law firm, at an office party and they struck up a conversation, and she found him pleasant and engaging. Before leaving, Ed asked Jane if he could call her. She said yes and gave him her unlisted number. He called her the following week and they made a date for dinner on Saturday evening. The dinner went well and Jane invited Ed back to her apartment for coffee.

There, after casual conversation, Ed reached out to Jane and tried to kiss her while they were seated together on the sofa. Jane moved away, telling him that it was late, she was tired, and wanted him to leave. She asked him several times to please leave. At these remarks, Ed appeared surprised, became agitated, and reached for Jane again, stating that he did not want to leave and that he wanted to have sex with her. Jane said "No" firmly, and pleaded with Ed to leave. However, Ed was much bigger and heavier than Jane, and as he held her arms tightly and spoke with such insistence, she observed an intense look in his eyes that scared her. She believed that if she tried to resist him physically, he would hurt her. Frightened, she relented, and offered no resistance when Ed engaged with her in sexual intercourse. Jane did not seek any medical or other assistance, and told no one about the encounter. The following Monday, feeling distraught and angry, she went to the police station to make a formal charge of rape against Ed. Based on her complaint, the police arrested Ed.

The prosecutor interviewed Jane. She gave a credible account of the event. The prosecutor, experienced in sex-crime prosecutions, questioned her very closely; there did not appear to be any motive for Jane to make a false accusation. Ed's lawyer discussed the case with the prosecutor. He acknowledged that his client did have sexual intercourse with Jane, but that it was consensual, and that Jane even called Ed the next day to tell him that she had a nice time. After confirming that a call had been made the next day from Jane's number to Ed, the prosecutor asked her about the call, which she had not mentioned during her initial interview with the prosecutor. Jane said that she felt humiliated, and angrily called Ed crying and asking how he could have done such a horrible thing to her. However, the prosecutor could find nothing in Ed's background or character that would suggest he was lying about the incident, nor anything in Jane's background or character that would suggest she was fabricating her account. There is no evidence, however, to corroborate her account.

The prosecutor believes Jane is telling the truth. However, the prosecutor has no basis other than Jane's accusation to disbelieve Ed. The prosecutor believes that a jury might very well convict Ed on the basis of Jane's testimony, there being sufficient proof of Jane's lack of consent, and proof of force, or threat of force. The prosecutor also knows from experience that juries are much more sensitive to charges of rape by nonstrangers, and are more likely to convict than ever before. Should the prosecutor institute charges against Ed of forcible rape? What degree of moral confidence should guide the prosecutor's decision?

Spousal Abuse and Self-Defense, the Story of Ella

Ella had been married to Don for six years. They had one child, Tina, who is five years old. During virtually the entire period of their marriage Don physically abused Ella. Don often drank excessively, and it was on these occasions that he would become most brutal. Ella summoned the police on several occasions when Don was out of control and the beatings were most violent, the last time being one week earlier. Ella went to the hospital after that beating. Police and medical records confirm these facts and describe Ella's injuries. Nevertheless, Ella was in love with Don and because of their long-standing relationship, and for the sake of their child, she never initiated criminal charges against Don, never sought a court order of protection, and never left the household. Following the periods of abuse, Don would cry and ask Ella to forgive him, which she always did until the evening in question in June.

That evening, Don was drinking heavily and while in a rage, he punched Tina in her head for spilling her milk. Don had never struck Tina so viciously. When Ella screamed at him and sought to intervene, Don struck Ella repeatedly on her head and body with a broom handle. He shouted that if Ella ever questioned his authority again, he would kill her. Ella in terror locked herself and Tina in the bathroom. Don left the apartment and returned two hours later, undressed, and went to bed. Ella, under emotional shock and confusion, went into the kitchen and obtained a knife.

She walked into the bedroom and stabbed Don in his chest, killing him. Ella immediately called the police and told them what happened. They arrested her on a charge of murder.

Ella's lawyer has informed the prosecutor of his client's version of the events. He has asked the prosecutor to review the report of Dr. David Wall, a highly respected clinical psychologist who has treated battered women, has written in scholarly journals about forensic issues concerning the "battered woman's syndrome," and has testified as an expert witness in numerous civil and criminal proceedings. Dr. Wall's report details the relationship between Ella and Don and provides considerable factual data for his conclusion that under the circumstances, on the night of the killing, Ella was in a state of shock, afraid for her life and that of her child, and believed that she and her child were in danger of being killed by Don. Dr. Wall concluded that Ella's belief under the circumstances was reasonable.

The prosecutor, from background and experience, is sensitive to issues of domestic violence. The prosecutor does not doubt that Ella believed that the only way to protect her life and that of her child was to take her husband's life. The prosecutor also has no reason to dispute Dr. Wall's conclusion that Ella was a battered victim who believed she had no other recourse than to kill her husband. The prosecutor knows from experience, however, that juries tend to reject the battered spouse syndrome as a defense to murder and would probably find Ella guilty. Juries logically might ask why Ella didn't simply leave the apartment with her daughter. At the time she stabbed her husband to death, she was in no imminent physical danger. If convicted, Ella would be subject to a mandatory sentence of fifteen years to life imprisonment. Should the prosecutor charge Ella with murder? What degree of moral confidence should guide the prosecutor's decision?

Jane's Case

The rape case is an extremely difficult charging challenge for a prosecutor. Although there is no corroboration of Jane's accusation, the prosecutor has considerable experience dealing with rape victims and believes Jane is telling the truth when she gives her dramatic description of misplaced trust, betrayal, and fear. The prosecutor is not able to detect the existence of any motive for Jane to fabricate her story. If the prosecutor is able to conclude to a very high degree of confidence—this standard is "moral certainty"—that Jane is telling the truth, then the prosecutor could properly charge Ed with rape.

However, the prosecutor's decision is much more difficult because based on her experience and intuition, she is aware of the possibility that both Jane and Ed could honestly believe that they are telling the truth. Their differing accounts concerning the issues of consent and force are not so widely divergent as to make this result implausible. And the nuances of speech, tone, and demeanor may have been sufficiently ambiguous to render their subjective interpretations of their interaction unclear.

The prosecutor, in weighing issues of credibility, should be wary of making predictions of how a jury might view the case. For example, if the prosecutor is morally certain that Ed raped Jane, the prosecutor should not be deterred from bringing the case in the belief that a jury might have a reasonable doubt of Ed's guilt. However, a prosecutor's assessment that a case is not strong and that a jury might have a reasonable doubt are certainly relevant factors in the prosecutor's charging decision. To be sure, some prosecutors refuse to try a case if they fear they will lose it. Some prosecutors are concerned about their won-lost record and how they will be viewed by their office and the public. However, an acquittal is often an ambiguous result. Depending on the case, it may be seen by the office and the public as a demonstration of prosecutorial integrity and a commitment to protecting the rights of crime victims. By the same token, it may also be viewed as a sign of incompetence, vindictiveness, and a waste of prosecutorial resources. An acquittal may also engender public cynicism in the ability of the criminal justice system to render justice, and thereby dissuade rape victims from coming forward with complaints.

On balance, if the prosecutor is morally uncertain whether the encounter was consensual, or whether Ed used sufficient force or threat of force to accomplish his purpose, the prosecutor should not charge Ed with rape. Jane was clearly in fear, and Ed used some degree of force. He was no doubt persistent in seeking Jane's consent, and Jane's subjective evaluation of the likelihood of harm is a relevant factor. Whether Ed used the degree of force necessary to transform the encounter into a rape is the moral question that is central to the prosecutor's charging decision.

The prosecutor should not charge Ed with forcible rape if she lacks moral certainty that Ed used sufficient force or threats to satisfy the legal elements of rape. There is no question that Jane's compelling account of the events might cause a jury to convict Ed, but this eventuality would violate the prosecutor's duty to seek justice and the possibility that an innocent person might be convicted. The prosecutor's decision not to charge rape might be unpopular; the prosecutor might be charged with sexism. It is hard to imagine that the prosecutor's explanation to Jane would be convincing.

Ella's Case

Unlike the rape case, Ella's killing of her husband Don presents no dispute about the facts. The prosecutor must resolve a strictly legal question: whether or not Ella can successfully claim that she was legally justified in killing her husband in light of the facts. Under the traditional theory of self-defense, a killing is justified if the defendant reasonably believes that using deadly force is necessary to protect herself or another person from the imminent use of deadly force. But how could Don threaten Ella with the imminent use of deadly force if he was asleep? Why did Ella not leave her apartment? Even if Ella honestly believed that she needed to kill Don to protect herself and her daughter, should the prosecutor not charge Ella with murder, nonetheless?

Most prosecutors probably would conclude that the claim of self-defense is not applicable under the circumstances and Ella would likely be charged with murder. However, prosecutors with experience in domestic violence complaints who have studied the legal and scholarly literature of spousal battering, together with Dr. Wall's expert conclusions, might find it morally difficult to charge Ella with murder. A more likely position would be that of a prosecutor who is morally uncertain as to the scope of the justification defense as it relates to Ella's case. The prosecutor may conclude that Ella honestly believed that her life was endangered by Don, but that she had other alternatives than to kill him. The prosecutor undoubtedly could locate an expert witness to support that view. The prosecutor, based on her experience, could conclude that a jury would also support that view, and a judge would be required to impose a substantial mandatory sentence. However, the prosecutor also knows that thousands of battered women throughout the country are incarcerated in prison under substantial sentences for crimes similar to Ella's.

This author's conclusion is that Ella should not be charged with murder. Even if she unreasonably believed her life was imminently threatened by Don, the honesty her belief under the circumstances should make the prosecutor morally uncertain whether justice would be served by charging her with murder. The prosecutor should look to other charging options—either not charging Ella at all, or charging her under a lesser degree of homicide such as manslaughter based on her honest but unreasonable belief that killing her husband was necessary to protect herself and her child. The charge would be based on the prosecutor's assessment of Ella's conduct, the harm she caused, the degree of blameworthiness of her conduct, the impact of a prosecution on deterring domestic violence, and the impact of a prosecution on the public's perception of the prosecutor's commitment to fairness and impartial justice in domestic violence cases.

Prosecutor Discretion Run Amok—the Case of Lee Carroll Brooker

Lee Carroll Brooker, a seventy-six-year-old decorated and disabled combat war veteran living in Alabama, was sentenced to die in prison for growing marijuana in his backyard. He grew the marijuana to alleviate the pain from his physical disabilities. The courts that imposed and affirmed his sentence acknowledged that his sentence was excessive and unjustified, but that their hands were tied by the state's mandatory sentencing laws. Even though marijuana for medical use was legal in twenty-three states and the District of

Columbia, it was still a serious felony in Alabama, where Brooker was convicted, and given the fact that Brooker had several robbery convictions when he was a young man in Florida, the marijuana conviction subjected him as a prior felony offender to the mandatory sentence of life imprisonment without parole.

In examining Brooker's ordeal, one might logically focus on the shockingly harsh punishment he received for such a relatively minor and nonviolent offense. In fact, Brooker petitioned the U.S. Supreme Court to review his sentence, claiming it was so excessive as to violate the Eighth's Amendment's ban on the infliction of cruel and unusual punishments. However, the Supreme Court declined to review his sentence, which is not much of a surprise given how rarely the court reviews nondeath penalty sentences. Critics who study abuses in the criminal justice system would decry such an unconscionable sentence, its mandatory nature, and the dysfunctional legal system that would tolerate such excess and bar judges from modifying such inhumane treatment, but focusing on the system, the judges, and the punishment misses the real point.

Indeed, Brooker would likely be a free man today, and there would be no debate over the harshness of his incarceration for life had the district attorney in the town where Brooker resided simply exercised sound, civilized, and humane judgment. The district attorney did not.

Surely a prosecutor's application of criminal statutes to a defendant's conduct could produce a variety of criminal charges and potential sentences. A rigid application of the legal rules could produce the kind of charging and sentencing decision that the local prosecutor exercised on Brooker. A more flexible approach by a fair and enlightened prosecutor seeking to temper justice with mercy could have produced a much more sensible charge and sentence. The point is that every key decision in the criminal justice system—especially the charging decision—rests on the prosecutor's discretion and the way in which the prosecutor exercises that discretion.

As the Brooker case demonstrates, the prosecutor's charging decision is the most formidable decision in the criminal justice process; it becomes the foundation for the potential deprivation of a defendant's liberty and sometimes even his life. The prosecutor's exercise of discretion is not only the heart of the prosecutor's function, it is the foundation for the operation of the criminal justice process itself. Indeed, the prosecutor's charging decision involves the most enormous exercise of power of any government official, aptly described by Supreme Court Justice Robert H. Jackson as "the most dangerous power of the prosecutor." Moreover, the prosecutor's charging power is virtually unreviewable. In a case such as Brooker's, where the recidivist charge carries a mandatory sentence of life in prison without parole, the prosecutor can unilaterally decide to bring such a charge and a court has no power to review it or rectify that decision, however unjust it might be. Given the numerous factors that go into a prosecutor's exercise of discretion, it is exceedingly difficult to formulate precise standards to guide and limit a prosecutor's charging function, even assuming that prosecutors would follow those standards.

Was the Alabama prosecutor legally mandated to charge Brooker with the most serious drug felony? Was he required to then ratchet up the charge by adding Brooker's prior felony convictions to deem him a repeat offender subject to the mandatory sentence of life without parole? Of course not. Consider the facts in Brooker's case. The police seized thirty-four marijuana plants from his yard which weighed 2.85 lbs. in their entirety, including the large unusable stalks, whose weight was above the threshold of 2.2 lbs. for a Class A felony drug charge, the most serious drug charge. Combining that drug charge with Brooker's prior felonies allowed the prosecutor to invoke the mandatory life without parole sentence.

But of course, as the prosecutor well knew, the maximum amount of usable marijuana from the plants seized was only a tiny fraction of the 2.85 lbs., and certainly well under the 2.2 lbs. threshold for a Class A felony. Knowing this, did the prosecutor have to consider the highest weight, even though the prosecutor knew it was obviously an artificial weight? And given the artificiality of the weight, could not the prosecutor have exercised discretion to charge a lower weight, and thereby bring a reduced drug charge that did not carry a mandatory sentence? Since there was no evidence that Brooker was distributing the marijuana commercially—usually a good reason for a prosecutor to bring higher drug charges—could not the prosecutor, in exercising sound discretion, have sought to mitigate the harshness of bringing the highest drug charge by considering other critical factors, such as Brooker's use of the drug for personal health reasons, his distinguished military record, and the fact that Brooker's other felonies were committed over thirty years ago, when he was a troubled alcoholic as a young man?

Brooker was convicted by a jury; he refused to plead guilty. Did the prosecutor get the jury to convict Brooker of the most serious drug charge to retaliate against him for refusing to plead guilty? Do prosecutors actually retaliate against defendants when they refuse to plead guilty? It appears that prosecutors routinely do that. As former federal judge John Gleeson recently observed, prosecutors indeed do use their vast charging and sentencing powers to coerce defendants to plead guilty, with the most dire consequences if they refuse; "sentences so excessively severe they take your breath away," Judge Gleeson observed. He described the prosecutor's power to inflict overly harsh punishments, often for minor drug offenses, as a legal "sledgehammer," and a "two-by-four to the forehead."

Responsibility for the problem of mass incarceration in the United States has been attributed to many causes, but I would suggest that one of the principal reasons why so many offenders, especially minor drug offenders, are in U.S. prisons for such stunningly long terms is because of the prosecutor's charging and sentencing power.

In the end, the integrity of the criminal justice system is eroded and too many minor offenders live and die in jail because some prosecutors behave with callous indifference to the real-life consequences of their actions.

Alabama now allows limited use of marijuana for medical reasons. However, Lee Carroll Brooker, seventy-six years old, remains in prison.

The Tragic Story of Aaron Swartz and the "By the Book" Federal Prosecutors

Aaron Swartz was celebrated as the twenty-six-year-old Internet folk hero and crusader who sought to make Internet Web files free and open to the public. Dubbed "the humanist hacker," Swartz was indicted in 2011 by federal prosecutors on numerous counts of computer and wire fraud for breaking into computer networks at the Massachusetts Institute of Technology and using a false account to download some 4.8 million academic documents from the JSTOR database. The charges carried a potential punishment of thirty-five years in jail and a $1 million fine. Swartz committed suicide a few months before he was to stand trial. His death evoked tidal waves of outrage against the federal prosecutors for vastly abusing their power by bringing inflated and unfair charges.

The government's conduct has been called a "grotesque miscarriage of justice," "egregious overcharging," and "shameless." The vitriol against the prosecutors is not surprising. The pursuit of Swartz appears to have been Javert-like; it involved expending considerable legal resources, bringing draconian felony charges against a person whom the prosecutors knew was emotionally fragile and possibly suicidal, and with the certain awareness by the prosecutors that Swartz was motivated not by greed or self-interest but by principled idealism. To Swartz's defenders, the prosecutors' conduct appears to run absolutely counter to the conventional understanding that a prosecutor's legal and ethical responsibility is not to tack scalps onto his wall but to serve justice.

Unfortunately, there is more to this tragic story. Vilifying prosecutors in this way occurs every time a prosecutor uses his or her enormous discretion to bring criminal charges that in many instances may be seen as abusive, overzealous, and unjust. Indeed, there are hundreds and hundreds of cases in which prosecutors, as in the Aaron Swartz case, have been accused of this type of arbitrary, vindictive, and tyrannical behavior. Many of these cases illustrate the way a prosecutor can use vague, broadly worded, and open-ended statutes such as the Computer Fraud and Abuse Act to charge crime.

But for those who are quick to accuse the prosecutors with overzealous behavior, it is important to understand what the Swartz case is not about. It is not about selecting

Swartz from a group of similarly situated individuals, many of whom may have violated a law, and then prosecuting only him and not the others. That was the accusation against prosecutors when they massed their heavy firepower to single out and prosecute Martha Stewart, who did lie to federal officials, and her act did violate federal law. The Swartz case is not about a prosecutor retaliating against someone because that person engaged in constitutionally protected activity, such as protesting, whistle-blowing, or associating with unpopular groups. Even Swartz's most ardent supporters do not contend that his conduct was constitutionally protected.

There is no suggestion that the government targeted Swartz for prosecution based on personal or political reasons, or as part of a vendetta against political foes, as in the federal prosecution of former Alabama governor Don Siegelman, covered later in this chapter. From reviewing the criminal charges, it appears that in gaining access to the networks dishonestly, Swartz did in fact commit acts that were unlawful under the statute. There is nothing to suggest that the prosecutors in his case behaved with improper motives or violated any legal or ethical rules.

For prosecutors to charge an individual who openly violates the law and is so outspoken about his unlawful conduct is hardly exceptional or surprising. Indeed, any responsible prosecutor could reasonably be expected to bring charges against that person as a deterrent to discourage other potential offenders from committing similar crimes. Channeling a prosecutor's discretion in this way is well within the legitimate contours of prosecutorial decision-making, particularly for those prosecutors who are specially assigned to investigate and prosecute electronic crimes as these prosecutors were. Also, not to be ignored—and I'm sure it had some influence on the decision to charge Swartz—is the fact that in 2008 Swartz created a program to enable him to access and download data from a massive federal court database of over 20 million pages of federal judicial documents. To a prosecutor who believes in good faith that he or she has the responsibility to vindicate the law, prosecute an open and notorious cyber-violator, and thereby deter other potential violators, charging Swartz or anyone else is neither illegitimate, irresponsible, nor surprising.

To be sure, the fact that a prosecutor has good cause to believe that somebody committed a crime does not mean that the prosecutor necessarily should charge that person, nor does it mean that a prosecutor should bring charges that are disproportionate to the offense. What is so troubling about the Swartz case is the realization that a prosecutor—federal or state—has almost unlimited power to decide whether someone should be charged with a crime, how serious the charge should be, and whether to give that person any leniency. A prosecutor's charging power is the most dangerous power of all because it can be so easily abused, and there are virtually no checks to correct abuses.

The tragic case of Aaron Swartz unquestionably is one of the most troubling recent examples of a prosecutor's use of his broad discretion to charge crime. Indeed, the circumstances of Swartz's case appear to allow, if not invite, heavy overcharging. The computer fraud statute is extremely broad, violating the statute is not too difficult, and violators are either never detected or are not prosecuted because of lack of resources or other law enforcement priorities.

In the end, the single most significant check on a prosecutor's discretion is neither the judicial courts nor the court of public opinion. The only realistic check lies in the integrity, professionalism, and sense of fair play by prosecutors. To those friends and supporters of Aaron Swartz, this assuredly will not be seen as much of a check.

The Nonprosecution of Lance Armstrong

Lance Armstrong was stripped of his seven Tour de France titles, numerous endorsements, and banned from cycling and Olympic competition for life. He was exposed as a fake, a cheater, and a mean-spirited bully. Proof that Armstrong was the ringleader of the biggest sports doping conspiracy ever is overwhelming. However, he escaped one major pitfall—he was not criminally charged for clearly prosecutable crimes in what antidoping officials called "the most sophisticated doping program in history." Why did Armstrong escape criminal prosecution?

The U.S. Justice Department investigated Armstrong in 2010 after cyclist Floyd Landis, another Tour de France winner and former teammate of Armstrong's on the U.S. Postal Service team, blew the whistle on Armstrong's extensive drug use. Landis reported that Armstrong conspired with other teammates on how to use drugs and avoid detection, and Armstrong's use of guile and threats to keep others silent. Dozens of witnesses, including many of the most famous riders on Armstrong's team, testified before a federal grand jury about the widespread fraudulent scheme and drug trafficking conspiracy but the federal investigation was abruptly halted by the U.S. attorney in Los Angeles without any explanation. Agents involved in the investigation reportedly were stunned and furious that the case was dropped. There appears to be no credible reason why the prosecutor decided to terminate the investigation.

The obvious question is whether a prosecutor can simply stop an ongoing investigation without giving any reason? Doesn't the public have a right to know why a famous athlete who appears to have committed serious crimes is being let off even though there appears to be abundant evidence to prove his wrongdoing? Can an individual force a prosecutor to act? Can a court? Can a grand jury?

The law is very clear: a prosecutor's power to bring criminal charges also includes the power to not bring charges. In fact, a prosecutor's discretion to decline to bring charges may be more controversial than a prosecutor's discretion to affirmatively bring charges. That is because the basis for the decision not to charge is far more unknowable than the decision to bring charges. The prosecutor's decision to bring charges involves much more transparency because the basis for that decision may be illuminated by the evidence, the rules of discovery, motions to dismiss, and ultimately a criminal trial. If a prosecutor decides not to prosecute a case, however, there is no way to know why the prosecutor refused to act, unless the prosecutor publicly announces his or her reasons. An individual has no power to force a prosecutor to bring charges. A court may not compel a prosecutor to proceed in a case that a prosecutor believes does not warrant a prosecution.

Indeed, even a grand jury cannot compel a prosecutor to bring charges. In a famous case occurring during the civil rights battles of the 1960s, *United States v. Cox*, a federal district judge in Mississippi held the prosecutor in contempt for refusing to sign an indictment voted by a federal grand jury against two civil rights activists. The Fifth Circuit Court of Appeals reversed the citation, stating that a prosecutor's discretion not to sign or prosecute an indictment cannot be coerced or reviewed by the courts. This refusal to compel prosecution is based on the constitution's Separation of Powers, which means that courts are not allowed to micromanage the way prosecutors in the Executive Branch do their jobs.

One can only speculate on why the U.S. attorney declined to prosecute Armstrong despite what appears to be powerful evidence of conspiracy, fraud, doping, and obstruction of justice. Perhaps the acquittal of Roger Clemens on charges that he lied to Congress about using steroids, or the ambiguous verdict in the Barry Bonds trial in which a jury convicted Bonds of the weakest count of obstruction of justice by giving evasive answers to a grand jury about whether he used performance-enhancing drugs, might have persuaded the Justice Department that it had run its course on trying to prosecute elite athletes for using drugs. The Justice Department may also have been smarting over the recent acquittal of vice-presidential candidate John Edwards for campaign finance violations in a prosecution that many commentators saw as an overreach. The Justice Department may also have felt that Armstrong's iconic status as a cancer survivor who became a cycling champion and worldwide celebrity may have made a successful prosecution much more difficult.

Speculation is simply that. The failure of the prosecutor to explain his reasons for nonprosecution likely breeds cynicism and makes the public distrust the fairness and impartiality of the criminal justice system. Surely, a prosecutor's decision not to prosecute may be the result of a good faith evaluation of the evidence, the need to conserve scarce resources, and the risks of losing an important case. However, the decision may also be made in bad faith, for corrupt or other improper reasons, but the public will never know why because prosecutors are not required to give reasons. While people may speculate and wonder why, the question of whether Lance Armstrong escaped criminal prosecution for proper reasons or improper reasons will never be known

Prosecution and Politics, the Case of Don Siegelman

No case illustrates a prosecutor's abuse of discretion better than the U.S. Department of Justice's politically driven prosecution of Don Siegelman. In 2002, Siegelman, a Democrat, was the elected governor of the blood-red state of Alabama and was predicted to win reelection. According to sworn and strongly corroborated testimony before the House Judiciary Committee, Alabama's top Republican operative Bill Canary contacted Karl Rove, President George Bush's most powerful advisor, and instigated the Justice Department's prosecution of Siegelman. Rove contacted the Department of Justice's Public Integrity Section, and Canary declared confidently that "his girls would take care of Siegelman." When asked who "his girls" were, Canary replied Alice Martin, the U.S. attorney for the Northern District of Alabama, and Leura Canary, the U.S. attorney for the Middle District of Alabama. Leura Canary, by the way, is Bill Canary's wife.

Rumblings about the Justice Department's investigation of Siegelman permeated the media, and cost Siegelman his reelection, but by a hair; Republican Bob Riley prevailed by a few thousand votes, mysteriously discovered in a polling place in a rural county vacated by Democratic poll watchers after the polls closed. Siegelman, polls showed, was heavily favored to win a rematch against any Republican opponent. That was before federal prosecutors ratcheted up their hunt.

First, Alice Martin, one of Bill Canary's "girls," indicted Siegelman in 2004 for bid-rigging on state contracts. But that indictment was thrown out almost as quickly as it was brought by Federal District Judge U. W. Clemon, the most senior judge in Alabama. Judge Clemon, in dismissing the indictment for lack of evidence, wrote that the prosecution "was completely without legal merit" and in a further remarkable statement, said that the prosecution of Siegelman "was the most unfounded criminal case over which I presided in my entire judicial career."

However, Bill Canary's other "girl," his wife Leura, had much better success. Her office indicted Siegelman for numerous RICO violations and a bribery count for accepting a large donation to a state lottery campaign to fund free tuition for high school graduates and appointing the donor to a seat on the state medical board, a position he had held under three previous administrations. The bribery charge was the first bribery case ever brought by the Justice Department predicated on an issue-advocacy campaign contribution in which the alleged beneficiary, Siegelman, received not one penny.

There was another big difference in the two prosecutions—a different federal judge. Presiding over the Canary prosecution was Judge Mark Fuller, who according to sworn testimony before the House Judiciary Committee, was handpicked by the Justice Department to "hang Don Siegelman." Fuller had been investigated by Siegelman for financial fraud when Siegelman previously was Alabama's attorney general.

The jury deliberated for eleven days, telling the judge several times that it was "hopelessly deadlocked," but was forced to continue deliberating and ultimately found Siegelman guilty of the single bribery count, acquitting him of all twenty-two RICO counts.

The bribery conviction rested on a questionable legal instruction given to the jury by Judge Fuller that omitted one of the key legal requirements to convict of bribery—the need for an explicit promise or understanding. Indeed, it would not be too far-fetched to suggest that under Judge Fuller's deficiently worded instruction, every U.S. president who ever appointed as an ambassador a wealthy donor who contributed heavily to the president's campaign conceivably would be guilty of bribery.

And what was the basis for the inclusion in the indictment of the incendiary RICO corruption counts—all twenty-two of them? The jury acquitted because proof was completely nonexistent. Indeed, it reasonably appears that the motive of the federal prosecutors in including the RICO counts in the indictment was for the exact purpose of prejudicing the jury by portraying Siegelman as part of a corrupt conspiracy network and thereby improving their chances of getting a conviction on the bribery count.

Characterizing this case as "extraordinary," but deferring to the jury's verdict—which appellate courts invariably do—the Eleventh Circuit Court of Appeals upheld the verdict but ordered a hearing on two claims. One claim challenged Judge Fuller's astonishingly harsh sentence that dramatically increased the offense level to three times what the sentencing guidelines mandate—from a five-year sentence to a fifteen-year sentence. The second claim related to the "Canary Connection." When news of her husband's possible involvement in Siegelman's prosecution surfaced, Leura Canary was disqualified from being part of the prosecution because of her obvious conflict of interest.

It was subsequently revealed that despite her disqualification, she remained heavily involved in the investigation and prosecution of Siegelman. Indeed, her continued involvement violates a fundamental precept in American criminal law: that a prosecutor must remain impartial and disinterested in the prosecution of a case. She had a direct personal and political interest in the success of her husband's client—the Republican candidate for governor—and in Siegelman's electoral defeat.

Ruling on a posttrial motion, Judge Fuller rejected the claim that Canary participated in the Siegelman prosecution, but in Humpty-Dumpty fashion, he denied Siegelman the opportunity to discover evidence in the prosecution files that could prove he was prejudiced by her continued involvement. Among the items of proof offered by Siegelman to prove Canary's continued involvement in the Siegelman prosecution are the following:

> Canary e-mailed members of the Siegelman prosecution team as they were preparing a superseding indictment and advising them that Siegelman and his campaign supporters conducted a survey showing that 67 percent of Alabama voters believed the prosecution of Siegelman was politically motivated, advising that "perhaps grounds not to let him discuss court activities in the media?" Following this e-mail the prosecution sought in its very first pretrial motion an order prohibiting Siegelman from presenting evidence, testimony, or argument "that politics was a motivating factor in the government's decision to prosecute" him, adding that "for months Siegelman has inundated the media with accusations that his prosecution is the result of a political witch hunt."
>
> Members of the prosecution team noted that Canary approved the assignment of a particular employee to work on the Siegelman case.
>
> An employee in Canary's office—Tamara Grimes—alleged that Canary maintained direct communication with the prosecution team, directed actions in the case, and monitored the case through members of the prosecution team and the first assistant U.S. attorney.

> Canary rewarded with a personal acknowledgment every milestone in the Siegelman case. She also hosted a gala party at a fancy restaurant when the superseding indictment was unsealed. She hosted a similar celebration when Siegelman was convicted.
>
> Canary and the first assistant wrote all the press releases in the case under the signature of acting U.S. attorney Franklin. Canary's close associates in the office communicated Canary's suggestions to the acting U.S. attorney. Grimes, the employee who blew the whistle on Canary's continued involvement, was subjected to retaliation by Canary and others.

Respected observers from both political parties have condemned the legality of Siegelman's prosecution on numerous grounds. Over one hundred former attorney generals from both political parties have decried the legal and ethical irregularities that contaminated the Siegelman prosecution, as have widespread commentary from journalists, academics, and disinterested observers. Former Arizona attorney general Grant Woods, a Republican, stated: "This was a Republican state and Siegelman was the one Democrat they could never get rid of." Former Alabama U.S. attorney Doug Jones stated: "It appeared that government agents were not investigating any allegations of a crime, but were fishing around for anything they could find against Siegelman." Former Republican Congressman from Alabama Parker

Griffith called the Siegelman prosecution a "political assassination."

The prosecution of Don Siegelman may have been the most unjust "corruption" prosecution ever brought by the Justice Department, ranking much higher than several other recent inept and misguided prosecutions—late Senator Ted Stevens, John Edwards, the River Birch defendants in New Orleans, and the Alabama casino operators. It is unknown why President Obama refused to grant Siegelman a pardon or commute his sentence. It certainly takes a certain amount of political courage to grant a pardon or commute a sentence, and put some type of closure to a misguided prosecution.

Whatever the legacy of this misbegotten case, there is one dramatic lesson for anyone interested in how federal criminal justice can break down. The Siegelman case shows how the worst in partisan politics, mixed with irresponsible and overzealous prosecution, can make a poisonous brew that produces cruel justice.

Federal Judge Mark Fuller resigned from the bench on August 1, 2015, after he was arrested and charged with battery of his wife. His resignation avoided impeachment proceedings to remove him.

On February 1, 2017, one month after President Barack Obama declined his pardon application, Don Siegelman was quietly released from federal prison. He served over six years.

Chapter Two

The Prosecutor and the Grand Jury

A Cooperative Team

The grand jury is a part of law enforcement that is not well understood by the public. The right to have a grand jury institute charges is listed in the Constitution, and in early common law was seen as a core protection against a tyrannical government. Today, however, the grand jury has no real independent power but functions together with and under the control of the prosecutor. Indeed, the prosecutor determines whether a grand jury will be empaneled, what matters the grand jury will consider, and what decisions the grand jury will make. Thus, when one reads a headline of actions taken by a grand jury, such as issuing subpoenas, summoning witnesses, investigating a crime, holding a witness in contempt, or returning an indictment, one must realize that these are not the actions of the grand jury acting independently; they are the actions of the prosecutor acting in the name of the grand jury.

The power of the grand jury as a tool of the prosecutor is described in the following stories. The stories reflect in different ways how prosecutors may use grand juries for legitimate purposes, and may misuse grand juries for illegitimate purposes. Although there are calls from time to time to abolish grand juries, or make the process more transparent, it is unlikely that the powers of such a critical law enforcement institution will be significantly limited any time soon. Some tinkering around the edges is possible, such as altering the rules of grand jury secrecy and allowing lawyers for some witnesses to appear inside the grand jury room, but the overall power of the grand jury, acting in tandem with a powerful prosecutor, is unlikely to be curtailed.

A Tool of Tyranny

From many years of experience before grand juries, I am confident in stating that the grand jury is the most powerful instrument in the arsenal of law enforcement. Historically, the grand jury was considered a buffer between the government and the individual, an accuser of the guilty, and a protector of the innocent. Today, however, there is an unmistakable emphasis on ex parte investigation and accusation as opposed to exoneration. Judge Learned Hand famously said this about the grand jury: "Save for torture, it would be hard to find a more effective tool of tyranny than the power of unlimited and unchecked ex parte examination." Judge Hand was correct. There is no comparable agency in criminal law enforcement with a greater potential to abuse power than a grand jury operating in tandem with a prosecutor.

The grand jury and the prosecutor enjoy an unusually close and mutually reinforcing relationship. The prosecutor empanels grand juries, initiates grand jury investigations, summons and interrogates witnesses before grand juries, subpoenas documents, gives the grand jury its legal instructions, and recommends the actions he wants the grand jury to take. The grand jury is totally dependent on the prosecutor for its day-to-day operations, which typically involves hearing witnesses testify and voting indictments. Exonerations are infrequent. Close observers of grand juries, including many judges, claim that any experienced prosecutor could indict almost anybody at any time for almost anything before any grand jury. Although this may be an exaggeration, it is not very far from the truth.

The grand jury's investigative power is breathtakingly broad and has consistently been reaffirmed by the courts. The modern grand jury is empowered to summon any person before it and subject to very modest constraints, to compel that person to disclose under oath everything he or she knows about the matter under inquiry. The witness is required to answer every question asked, and is not allowed to challenge the relevancy or competency of the questions asked or the power of the grand jury to ask the questions. It is therefore not surprising that the rights of witnesses before grand juries are extremely limited. A witness has no right to remain silent, no right to have the assistance of counsel inside the grand jury room, and no right to be told that they are targets of the grand jury's investigation.

The ability of prosecutors to intimidate grand jury witnesses is borne out by numerous cases. One case that quickly comes to mind involved an investigation by a grand jury of a state senator for corruption. The focus of the probe was on the relationship between the senator and a wealthy real estate developer based on information that the developer made large financial contributions to the senator's reelection campaign in return for the senator's help so that the developer could avoid onerous licensing, construction, and development requirements. The senator was an attorney and was allowed to maintain a private law practice as per the rules of the senate.

The prosecutor served grand jury subpoenas on the senator, his law firm, and his staff, ordering the production of numerous documents related to the senator's law practice and senatorial work. The prosecutor sought to question the senator's chief of staff about several encounters between the senator and the developer in which the construction project was discussed. The prosecutor advised the chief of staff that he was not a target of the investigation, but he refused to testify. The prosecutor then gave him immunity to compel his testimony. The prosecutor advised him that even with immunity, his refusal to answer any questions would subject him to punishment for contempt, and that if he lied he would be charged with perjury and obstruction of justice.

The senator's chief of staff testified that he did not recall any conversations with the senator related to any financial arrangements with the developer. The witness was shown an e-mail he wrote immediately after one of the meetings and was asked again to recount the meeting. The witness again stated he did not remember the meeting. Speaking in a very loud voice, the prosecutor stated: "You know you're lying"; "Don't insult this jury"; "You'll be held in contempt and thrown in jail unless you tell this grand jury the truth"; "You'll never work again." The witness stood up, told the prosecutor he would not continue to be abused by his threats and bullying, and walked out of the grand jury room. The prosecutor ordered the grand jury to return an indictment charging the witness with criminal contempt.

The defendant's motion to dismiss the indictment on grounds of prosecutorial misconduct was denied. The court found that the prosecutor's treatment of the witness, while somewhat harsh, was a legitimate means of trying to get the witness to cooperate, especially since the prosecutor had made a strong showing that the witness was deliberately trying to impede the grand jury's investigation.

This example is not atypical. The defendant was convicted and imprisoned for twelve months. The senator was also convicted and sentenced to three years imprisonment.

Did the Prosecutors of Julius and Ethel Rosenberg Suborn Perjury?

The recently disclosed grand jury testimony of David Greenglass, the government's star witness in the 1951 espionage trial of "Atom Spy" defendants Julius and Ethel Rosenberg, raises new questions about whether the prosecutors suborned perjury. The Rosenbergs were convicted and executed in Sing Sing's Electric Chair. The proof against Julius Rosenberg was strong but the proof against his wife Ethel was weak; her guilt hinged mainly on the testimony of Greenglass, her brother.

Greenglass's grand jury testimony was released by Federal District Judge Alvin K. Hellerstein following a lawsuit by archivists, historians, and journalists to unearth additional material about one of the most famous and controversial criminal trials in U.S. history. Greenglass died last year, which allowed his testimony to be made public under the terms of the lawsuit.

Absent from Greenglass's grand jury testimony, which he gave seven months before the trial, is any testimony, direct or indirect, that incriminates his sister, Ethel. Indeed, Greenglass testified that he "never spoke to Ethel about this at all," referring to Julius Rosenberg's delivery of atomic secrets to Russian agents. However, at the trial, Greenglass testified for the first time that Ethel typed her husband's handwritten notes for delivery to the Russians. In his summation, the prosecutor used her typing to argue, metaphorically, that

Ethel "struck the keys, blow by blow, against her own country in the interests of the Soviets."

However, decades later, Greenglass admitted to lying at the trial and falsely accusing his sister Ethel in order to protect his wife, Ruth. In his 2001 book, "*The Brother: The Untold Story of Atomic Spy David Greenglass and How He Sent His Sister, Ethel Rosenberg, to the Electric Chair*," Greenglass states that he was pressured by the prosecutors to commit perjury and that he did so in order to save his wife from prosecution. He suggests that his wife, rather than Ethel, had typed the notes. Although Greenglass's grand jury testimony does not directly contradict his trial testimony, it does omit critical facts about which he testified at the trial and which formed the basis for Ethel's conviction and execution. However, the fact that his testimony differed so dramatically from the grand jury to the trial reinforces his claim that the prosecutors suborned perjury.

There is no question that had Ethel's lawyers been aware of Greenglass's grand jury testimony, they could have used it quite effectively to impeach Greenglass's credibility. By confronting him with his grand jury testimony, in which he essentially absolved Ethel of any involvement in the espionage plot, and made no mention of her typing incriminating notes, Ethel's lawyers would have been able to suggest that his new testimony at the trial was given in exchange for the prosecution's agreement to show leniency to his wife and which, in fact, saved his wife from being charged. What happened that caused Greenglass to suddenly accuse his sister?

The federal prosecutors, Irving Saypol, Roy Cohn, and Myles Lane, are not around to answer. The most an observer can do is speculate on how it came to be that Greenglass pleaded guilty for a reduced sentence, changed his story from the grand jury to the trial to incriminate Ethel, and kept his wife from being charged. Did Greenglass's new account at trial result from his own newly refreshed memory of the events, or was he instigated and coached by the prosecutors to change his story to accuse Ethel, against whom there was virtually no other proof?

The prosecutors did not disclose Greenglass's grand jury testimony to the Rosenberg's lawyers. Did they have an obligation to do so? Today, the rules of evidence absolutely require prosecutors to disclose to the defense all prior statements of any witness called by the government that the defense may use upon cross-examination to attack that witness's credibility. Indeed, confronting a witness with his or her prior inconsistent statements, including significant omissions—as Greenglass's grand jury testimony certainly contained—is one of the most common techniques used to undermine a witness' credibility. The theory is that a witness who says one thing today but said something different yesterday is less trustworthy than a witness who is consistent in his recollections. Whether this theory is well-founded or not is debatable. Nevertheless, the ability of a lawyer to challenge a witness with his or her different account of an event may certainly help the jury evaluate that witness's truthfulness.

In 1951, a prosecutor was not required to disclose prior statements of a witness to the defense, and certainly not required to disclose secret grand jury testimony. However, at the time, there was one major exception: prosecutors then, as now, are constitutionally and ethically required to behave fairly, and not to strike "foul blows." Prosecutors then, as now, were admonished that they violate due process when they knowingly allow a witness to give false testimony. Prosecutors then, as now, were cautioned by the Canons of Professional Ethics that it is the primary duty of a prosecutor "to see that justice is done," and that "the suppression of facts capable of establishing the innocence of the accused is highly reprehensible."

If Greenglass's grand jury testimony is the truth, and if his later acknowledgment that he lied at the trial is also true, then Ethel Rosenberg was not proven to have had any part in the espionage plot and was wrongfully convicted and executed. In retrospect, the prosecution as a matter of fairness and justice had a duty to disclose Greenglass's grand jury testimony to the defense. Now, sixty-five years later, we have this new information to evaluate Greenglass's credibility, but the government had this information from the beginning.

We will probably never know exactly what the prosecutors did as the architects of the convictions and executions of Julius and Ethel Rosenberg. But it is more than troubling to believe that Cold War hysteria drove these prosecutors to engineer a prosecution that may have resulted in the conviction and execution of an innocent person.

The Grand Jury's Investigation of the Killing of Eric Garner

What can explain a Staten Island grand jury's refusal to indict New York City police officer Daniel Pantaleo for the chokehold death of Eric Garner? Even if the answer is speculative and inconclusive, asking the question is an appropriate and maybe cathartic effort—one that can help prosecutors address these difficult cases in a more effective way that inspires public confidence in the outcome.

The police confrontation with Garner, which was captured on video, is a powerful and horrifying image, especially to people who remember the violent beating of Rodney King by Los Angeles police in March 1991, also captured on video, and the riots that followed the jury's acquittal of those officers. The fact that the New York protests were relatively peaceful is a tribute to the good sense and restraint of New Yorkers, who while outraged at the grand jury's inaction, was taken in the hope that significant changes in police practices would be forthcoming.

Any effort to decipher the unknown numerical vote of the grand jury, reportedly composed of twelve whites and nine blacks and Hispanics, and why they voted the way they did, has to make some reference not simply to demographics but to the nature and politics of the community. Staten Island has long been considered an outlier among the other New York City boroughs, described as a "conservative bastion in a liberal city."

It is unclear whether that conservatism may have contributed to the grand jury's decision. What is clear, however, is the image of troubled race relations in Staten Island. A few years ago, the Department of Justice monitored racial tensions and police responses after the savage beating of a Mexican immigrant in the neighborhood of Port Richmond, and in 2008, there was a race-motivated election-night rampage, in which a group of white youths vented its anger at President Obama's election by brutally beating a black man with a metal pipe and police baton.

As a former prosecutor assigned to prosecute police misconduct cases, I am well aware of the attitudes that the public holds about police officers, especially as revealed by grand jurors and trial jurors asked to hold police officers criminally liable for their misconduct. Jurors are not very tolerant of police officers who take bribes, steal drugs, and lie. Jurors don't have to put themselves in a police officer's shoes to know that such conduct is dishonest, reprehensible, and should be punished. But jurors don't share this intolerance when it comes to an officer's use of force in encounters with possible wrongdoers who may be seen as endangering the police officer and others. Here, the juror is not being asked to assess the officer's honesty; he or she is being asked to assess the officer's judgment. In this situation, jurors tend not to second-guess the officer's often split-second judgment that a forceful response was required in a typically tense, volatile, and dangerous encounter. These jurors trust the police to protect their property, their well-being, and even their lives from violent predators in their community. When a police officer is accused of using excessive force, even lethal force, jurors and the general public typically give the officer the benefit of the doubt.

Because grand jury proceedings are secret, it is not known what Officer Pantaleo told the grand jury. He was the last witness, and a sense of what he said can be gleaned from the remarks of his lawyer, who likely prepared his testimony very carefully. One can assume that Pantaleo appeared contrite, even grief-stricken, at the death of Garner. He surely emphasized that it was never his intention to injure or harm anyone, and that at most it was a tragic accident, certainly not a crime. He probably acknowledged Garner exclaiming, "I can't breathe," because that was on the videotape. Pantaleo said, according to his lawyer, that he immediately disengaged and tried to get off Garner as quickly as he could. Pantaleo, according to his lawyer, downplayed any suggestion that he used a forbidden chokehold by stating that he employed a maneuver he learned at the police academy to try to "tip Mr. Garner off balance," but that he had to move his arm when they both fell to the ground, and he was in fear that he and Garner would go through a store window.

There are significant contradictions between Pantaleo's account (as described by his lawyer) and what is seen in the video. He appears in the video to remain atop Garner well after Garner, lying face down on the pavement with Pantaleo's arm wrapped around his neck, pleads that he can't breathe. Pantaleo's arm did not move off Garner's neck when they fell to the ground, as Pantaleo claimed. Presumably these contradictions, and other aspects of Pantaleo's story, would have been sharply probed and impeached by any responsible grand jury prosecutor. Facing the target of a grand jury investigation is an ideal opportunity for any prosecutor to grill the target on every aspect of his or her story in order to demonstrate to the grand jury that the story is not credible. Prosecutors do this routinely.

Did the Staten Island prosecutor treat Pantaleo's self-serving account with kid gloves, with leading and helpful questions? In New York, only the prosecutor can formally ask the court to unseal the proceedings and publish the transcripts. The Staten Island district attorney did not do so. Even though grand jury testimony is rarely released to the public, the fact that the public already saw the videotape of the fatal chokehold made this a perfect case for disclosure. However, despite considerable public interest in what happened inside the grand jury, a motion to unseal Pantaleo's grand jury testimony was denied by a lower court and upheld on appeal.

Complicating the grand jury's responsibilities is the fact that the homicide charges the jurors considered are difficult to understand and apply. None of them involved intentional conduct by the officer, so Pantaleo's plea before the grand jury that he did not intend to injure Garner is irrelevant. The critical mental states required for the degrees of unintentional homicide submitted to the grand jury involve recklessness and negligence. So, for example, for murder the jury would have to find that the officer acted with a "depraved indifference to human life," the type of wantonly reckless conduct that any person would know would almost certainly result in death. A good example would be a motorist who kills a pedestrian while driving one hundred miles an hour at high noon in Times Square. Manslaughter requires a showing of recklessness in which the actor is aware of and consciously disregards a substantial and unjustifiable risk of causing death. For example, the owner of a factory where a fatal fire has erupted who disregarded numerous safety violations, knew that the exits were locked, and knew that flammable substances in the factory could easily ignite. Finally, criminally negligent homicide requires proof not of recklessness but of criminal negligence, where the actor by his or her conduct—assume the person is intoxicated—fails to perceive a substantial and unjustifiable risk of causing death.

There is no question that Pantaleo's killing of Garner required the prosecutor to carefully instruct the grand jury on the crimes of unintentional homicide. With proper instructions, a grand jury could rationally decide not to indict the officer. However, the secrecy of the process is troubling. To protect the integrity of the criminal justice system, and the law enforcement officials who are responsible for making the system work, greater transparency would have been in the public interest. The court should have unsealed the grand jury proceedings to let the public know what happened.

The Grand Jury's Investigation of the Fatal Shooting of Michael Brown

A vivid example of a prosecutor's deviation from proper standards of conduct in presenting evidence to a grand jury and usurpation a grand jury's independence is the prosecutor's treatment of Police Officer Darren Wilson, who fatally shot Michael Brown in Ferguson, Missouri. The transcript of the proceedings, which was publicly released, shows that the prosecutors questioned Wilson in what appears to have been a calculated effort to exonerate him from criminal liability. They showed Wilson the kind of deference and indulgence that prosecutors almost never show to the target of an investigation. They went out of their way to forcefully present Wilson's defense of justification, to reinforce his account of being attacked by Brown, to evoke sympathy for Wilson, and to actually help Wilson explain his many omissions, inconsistencies, and contradictions.

The prosecutors never challenged his story, never confronted him with his prior contradictory statements and omissions, never questioned him over the implausibility of several parts of his story, never sought to impeach his credibility by confronting him with evidence that was inconsistent with his account, and never asked him about his own prior conduct involving the use of excessive force as they led Wilson through his narrative. The prosecutors did not question him about his own toxicology report that may have influenced his decision to use lethal force. Indeed, if one didn't know any better, one might think that Wilson was the prosecution's principal witness giving testimony against defendant Michael Brown.

Since the purpose of a grand jury investigation is to ascertain the truth about an alleged crime and the perpetrators, and to determine whether probable cause exists to seek an indictment, no responsible prosecutor acting in good faith would fail to inquire into clear and even obvious contradictions on critical issues in the case that might enhance the reliability of the proof. Thus, several parts of Wilson's account of the shooting were in conflict with other evidence, but the prosecutors never confronted him with these contradictions. Regardless of whether any witness's account may be credible, no responsible prosecutor would fail to question that witness about significant contradictions, unless the prosecutor is either inept, or deliberately seeks to hide or minimize them. Clearly, when significant contradictions are attributable to the target of the investigation, it is difficult to imagine a reasonable explanation for a prosecutor's failure to elicit these discrepancies, inconsistencies, contradictions, and omissions. The failure of a prosecutor to challenge the veracity or accuracy of the target of an investigation seriously compromises the integrity of the process.

According to Wilson's testimony, one of the significant reasons for Wilson to have stopped and investigated Brown was his having learned about a theft of cigarillos from a Ferguson market, and his belief that Brown matched the description of one of the perpetrators. In fact, Wilson's narrative of the encounter, the struggle, and his firing the fatal shots included vivid details of the possession of cigarillos by Brown, and how, in the volatile struggle in the car, Wilson was able to recall in such precise detail the hand with which Brown held the cigarillos, and how he transferred them from one hand to the other, all of this happening in a few seconds while they were struggling over Wilson's gun.

Regardless of whether Wilson's account was believable or not, it is difficult to understand why the prosecutors never confronted him with two prior statements he made to a police sergeant—the first statement moments after the shooting, and the second statement two weeks after the shooting—in which Wilson not only failed to mention anything about the theft of cigarillos, but stated positively on both occasions that he did not know anything about the market theft, or that cigarillos were taken, when he confronted Brown. According to the sergeant's testimony, based on his interviews with Wilson, he understood that the confrontation with Brown was "strictly about the sidewalk. It had nothing to do with Wilson investigating the stealing of cigarillos." Moreover, the sergeant also testified that Wilson never told him he chased Brown, that Brown was under the influence of some substance, and that Wilson was angry at being told to "fuck off," facts that the prosecutors emphasized in Wilson's testimony. Once again, regardless of whether Wilson was telling the truth, as a target of the inquiry of the investigation he should reasonably have been confronted by these discrepancies. The prosecutor's failure to do so is a serious deviation from proper and acceptable norms of grand jury practice.

It is noteworthy that despite knowing these significant discrepancies, the prosecutors not only refrained from questioning Wilson about them, but instead made a conscious effort to help him explain why he may have omitted these key facts. Indeed, it appears from the transcript that the prosecutors took at face value everything Wilson said, and made a deliberate effort to explain and reconcile his contradictions. Consider this exchange:

> Q. Would you say your conversation with the sergeant was kind of brief, not a lot of detail statement, would that be fair to say?
>
> A. Yeah, it was very brief.
>
> Q. Now, you know, I know you've probably thought about this every day since it's happened, would that be fair to say?

A. Yes.

Q. And do you think that after having really thought about this over time and basically you've had to tell this scenario a few times, do you think that if there are additional details that you may not give initially, do you think that's because you are putting so much thought into what happened or do you think that is things that maybe you kind of imagined happened, but didn't really happen, you understand my question?

A. Yeah.

Not only did the prosecutors fail to confront Wilson with significant contradictions, they went out of their way to bolster his version of the confrontation to make his version more plausible and justifiable. They humanized Wilson and thereby evoked sympathy from the grand jurors. After establishing that the area where the shooting took place was "volatile," "antipolice," "a lot of gangs," "a lot of violence," "a lot of gun activity," "and a lot of drugs," the prosecutors asked Wilson:

Q. Were you pretty much on high alert being in that community by yourself, especially when Michael Brown said, "Fuck what you say," I think you said?

A. Yes.

Q. You were on pretty high alert at that point knowing the vicinity and the area that you're in?

A. Yes.

The prosecutors went out of their way to bolster Wilson's honesty and candor, a practice that is unusual and counter what any responsible prosecutor would do. Consider the following:

> Q. And I guess to be fair about this, any time any law enforcement officer has asked to speak to you, you have willingly and voluntarily come in and been interviewed and answered all their questions, is that fair to say?
> A. Yes, ma'am.

The prosecutors' gentle and supportive treatment of Wilson is completely at odds with the way the prosecutors treated other grand jury witnesses whose accounts differed from Wilson's story and, if believed, would have supported a finding of probable cause against Wilson of unlawfully killing Brown. The prosecutors aggressively challenged the testimony of these other witnesses, stating that their testimony conflicted with the physical evidence and their own prior statements to the police. Prosecutors questioned Dorian Johnson, who was with Brown, in a manner to corroborate Wilson's account that Brown charged at Wilson before the fatal shot. When Johnson failed to testify the way the prosecutors wanted him to, they shifted focus and attempted to attack Johnson's character and background, something the prosecutors did not do when questioning Wilson, notwithstanding credible information that Wilson had used excessive force in the past and had been subject to prior civilian complaints.

The unbalanced treatment of the evidence is also shown by the prosecutors' use of toxicology evidence to try to show it had some relevance to Brown's conduct, but failed to introduce toxicology evidence that may have had relevance with respect to Wilson's conduct. Once again, this is not to assume that any of this evidence had any relevance; it is simply noteworthy to point out that the prosecutors did not present the evidence in a balanced manner.

Finally, there also was a concern that the district attorney, Robert McCullough, who supervised the grand jury inquiry, had a serious conflict of interest. Whether McCulloch was actually biased in favor of the police is unclear. However, McCullough's father was a police officer who was killed in the line of duty; McCullough was closely tied to a nonprofit group supporting families of police officers killed in the line of duty; and McCullough had made statements in a prior controversial police shooting that supported the police and disparaged the victims.

A grand jury is supposed to search for the truth. But given the unbalanced presentation of the evidence to the Ferguson grand jury, one might reasonably wonder whether McCulloch's background was relevant in trying to explain the process. To critics, it merely reinforced troubling questions about the integrity of the grand jury process and whether the prosecutors distorted the grand jury's ability to find the truth.

Chapter Three

Trial Stories

The Main Event

A criminal trial is the main event in American law. It is claimed to be a search for the truth about a unique historical event. For a prosecutor, the trial represents an opportunity to vindicate the rule of law and protect society by convicting and punishing wrongdoers. A trial happens only when a defendant refuses to voluntarily acknowledge his or her guilt through a guilty plea, which occurs over 95 percent of the time, and the prosecutor is then obliged to prove the defendant's guilt beyond a reasonable doubt. Although the judge administers the trial, the prosecutor in many ways is the producer, director, and star. He or she plays to an audience of jurors who observe the evidence—usually the testimonial performances of witnesses—and then process it before casting their fateful ballot. Some criminal trials are huge public spectacles, much like sporting events. A trial is indeed a battle between fierce adversaries that reaches a decisive, momentous, and sometimes tragic climax.

The prosecutor possesses all the evidence and directs how it plays out in the legal arena. The jury is the audience, but in contrast to a theater audience, a juror takes an oath to fairly and impartially decide whether the persons who occupy the witness stand are telling the truth. Jurors do this not only by listening to each witness's answers, but also by observing their tone of voice, gestures, mannerisms, and overall demeanor. As with a theater audience, jurors may not be aware of the extensive amount of time, effort, and suggestions made by the prosecutor in rehearsing a witness's testimony to mold, polish, and improve the performance. If an actor has performed his or her role successfully, the result may be an award for the actor, director, and show. If the witness has performed her role successfully, the result may be a victory for the prosecutor and the justice system. In contrast to a theater award, however, the prosecutor's victory has far more profound consequences: the community is made safer, and the defendant loses his liberty, and maybe even his life.

Coaching Witnesses, Creating Facts— The Conviction of Kenny Rupp

A criminal trial is supposed to be a search for the truth. If it is, then the prosecutor must ensure that his or her preparation of the testimony of witnesses promotes the communication of the truth, and not alters it. Preparing a witness to testify, while an accepted practice in the United States, is prohibited in many other countries. In places like the United Kingdom, for instance, it is considered unethical for a prosecutor or any lawyer even to contact a witness before the trial. Why? The danger is that a lawyer's contact with a witness might influence that witness's testimony. However, in an adversary system like the United States in which winning a case is the goal of every lawyer, such contact is allowed. In fact, most lawyers would probably acknowledge, with varying degrees of candor, that they do coach witnesses about what to say and how to say it, at least some of the time, and maybe all of the time.

Coaching has been called the "dark and dirty" secret of the U.S. adversary system. It is a practice that has given lawyers a reputation as purveyors of falsehoods. Coaching by prosecutors is even worse than coaching by private lawyers. The stakes are much higher in a criminal trial. Defendants can lose their reputation and liberty, and maybe their lives. A prosecutor, therefore, has a special responsibility as a minister of justice to protect the integrity of the fact-finding process and to make sure that in preparing a witness to testify, he or she does not influence the witness to alter the facts.

Witness preparation by prosecutors typically follows accepted protocols. In preparation for direct examination, the prosecutor may advise a witness of what to expect in the courtroom, where to sit, to speak clearly, and to wait for a question to be completed before answering. If the witness does not remember a fact, the prosecutor will advise the witness to say so. The prosecutor may review prior statements of the witness, ask open-ended questions initially, and then ask more specific questions after the witness has given a complete version of the event. If the witness forgets a fact, the prosecutor may try to stimulate the witness's memory by asking a leading question. If the witness's account differs from an account given by another witness, the prosecutor may ask questions to try to help the witness reconcile the contradiction, and may even indicate that the witness's prior statements are inconsistent with the statements of other witnesses, or that the witness's recollection of particular facts may be improbable. Even experienced prosecutors understand that how a question is asked, the tone that is used, suggestions or innuendos that accompany questions, the repetition of certain questions, and the number and persistence of follow-up questions, may tip off a witness to what the prosecutor expects the witness to say. The prosecutor knows that witnesses are nervous, view the prosecutor with respect, and have confidence in the prosecutor's expertise. Many witnesses are intimidated by the prosecutor. Thus, witnesses may be highly vulnerable to any cues and suggestions from the prosecutor as to what to say.

The prosecutor typically prepares the witness for cross-examination as well. The prosecutor will review any discrepancies with the witness's prior statements. If there are inconsistencies, the witness will be asked to explain them. A prosecutor will go over the witness's background and seek to have the witness recount anything in the past that might suggest that the witness has a motive to testify falsely against the defendant. The witness will be encouraged to acknowledge any past mistakes and to present his or her best recollection of the event.

The line between preparation and coaching is fuzzy. Consider the case of Kenny Rupp. On a muggy evening in June 2015, James Fox, a twenty-nine-year-old African-American man, was killed by four shotgun blasts fired from close range on a quiet neighborhood street. Fox's body was found lying in the gutter next to his parked car. Fox was a member of the "Satan Boys" street gang and the police surmised the killing was gang related. Josh Gordon, who lived on the block, told police he heard several loud cracks, looked out his ground floor kitchen window, and saw a man running down the block while carrying a long object. At the police precinct, Gordon was shown a series of photographs. He focused for several minutes on the photo of Kenny Rupp, a leader of the "Rattlesnakes" gang and a suspect in the case. Gordon stated: "I'm not sure but that looks like the person I saw."

Rupp was charged with Fox's murder. The assistant district attorney, Shiela Stone, in preparing the case for trial, interviewed Gordon. She told him that his testimony was critical to getting a conviction. The media had reported on the Rupp case and Gordon knew this. The prosecutor focused on Gordon's identification. She told him that it was the most important evidence in the case. Gordon repeated what he told the police: that Rupp looked like the person he saw running down the block. Prosecutor Stone told him that another witness had seen Rupp on the block moments before the shooting, but this was not true. She told Gordon about the local gang violence and that Rupp had a long criminal record related to gangs. She stressed that juries needed to hear strong, positive, and confident testimony from eyewitnesses, not "maybe," "I think," or "it's possible." She explained the layout of the courtroom, where people will be sitting, and noted that Rupp would be seated at the far table next to his lawyer.

Stone rehearsed Gordon's testimony several times, each time adjusting his answers to make him feel more comfortable and confident. She reminded him that when he was interviewed by the police he was undoubtedly very nervous. The final rehearsal went the best. As he was instructed by Stone, Gordon stated clearly where he was standing when he saw Rupp ("in my kitchen at the side of the window"), how far he was away from Rupp when he saw the defendant fleeing down the block ("less than twenty feet away"), how good a look he got ("an excellent look"), the lighting conditions ("the street was extremely well lit"), and his confidence that the person he saw running down the street was the defendant ("I'm absolutely positive").

Stone conducted a mock rehearsal of questions Gordon would likely be asked on cross-examination. Pretending to be the defense lawyer, she asked him aggressively: "Weren't you uncertain in the police station when the police asked you to make an identification?" ("No, I was nervous, but I was never uncertain"); "Didn't the police tell you to focus carefully on my client's photo?" ("No, they did not"); "The prosecutor rehearsed your testimony, didn't she?" ("No, she didn't rehearse my testimony. She went over my testimony. She told me to tell the truth.").

On the witness stand, Gordon gave an Oscar-winning performance. He answered all of Stone's questions clearly and confidently. The high point, of course, was when Stone asked Gordon to look around the courtroom and see if he recognized the person he saw running down the block carrying the long object. Gordon looked slowly around the courtroom. He looked at the audience. He looked at the jury box. Then he turned to look at the defense table. He stared directly at Rupp. He pointed his finger at Rupp and stated, "That's him. That's the man I saw running down the block." The prosecutor asked, "Are you certain?" "Yes. I'm positive," Gordon replied.

The cross-examination of Gordon did not even come close to undermining the accuracy of his identification. Stone had prepared Gordon well. He rebuffed all of the suggestions from defense counsel that he was confused by the police and intimidated by the prosecutor. He denied that he was anxious to assist law enforcement and give them the answers they wanted. He asserted confidently that his positive courtroom identification was based exclusively on his memory of the event and not from looking at photos or any other cues or suggestions by prosecutors or police.

Rupp was found guilty based on Gordon's positive courtroom identification. He was sentenced to life in prison without parole. Gordon was the only prosecution witness. There was no corroboration. The jury believed Gordon mostly because of the way Stone adjusted and polished Gordon's testimony. Stone, as would any film director, rehearsed Gordon's testimony carefully, but she did much more than that. She helped him improve the facts. Like a director, she provided an improvised rendition of the story and gave him suggestions and advice about demeanor, tone, and emphasis. Stone, like a film director, knew from years of experience how to have an actor relate to the audience—or a jury. When she asked Gordon, in an artificial but remarkably dramatic way, to look around the courtroom to see whether he recognized in the courtroom the armed gunman, Gordon performed on cue: he looked around the courtroom slowly and carefully, looked directly at Rupp, and pointed his finger straight at him, asserting dramatically, "That's him. That's the man I saw running down the street."

But Rupp was innocent. The real killer confessed four years later, and there was other evidence to strongly corroborate his guilt. Eyewitness mistakes account for the vast majority of wrongful convictions. Gordon's erroneous identification can be attributed in large part to Stone's preparation of Gordon's testimony. Her preparation was not unlike a director's preparation of an actor. Just as a director makes suggestions, gives cues, and offers critiques to adjust, polish, and improve the actor's performance, so did the prosecutor in preparing and shaping Gordon's testimony. Just as a director's input may result in a performance that is far different from the actor's initial rendition during an audition, so did the prosecutor's directions improve and even alter Gordon's original story. Just as a director tries to make the actor's performance "believable," so did the prosecutor.

Prosecutor Stone believed Rupp was guilty and prepared Gordon's testimony to prove his guilt. She believed she was serving justice by convicting a dangerous killer. But Stone's fixation on Rupp's guilt contributed not to justice, but to a miscarriage of justice.

Insanity on Trial

Trials have a way of opening windows into strange places. A case I prosecuted stands out.

Jonathan Hill was accused of the serial rape of at least seven women who ran dry cleaning establishments in upper Manhattan. There were other victims also, but they were too scared to come forward. Hill's method was consistent; he entered the store and forced the women at gunpoint to go a secluded area in the rear of the premises where he sexually assaulted them. Hill's identity was contained initially in a police sketch prepared by an artist from descriptions by the many women. Hill was later picked out from a police lineup by all of the women.

Hill was a huge man who stood over six feet, six inches tall and weighed over 300 pounds. Hill did not deny the rapes; he said he didn't remember them. He raised an insanity defense under which the prosecution would have to prove Hill's sanity beyond a reasonable doubt. His claim wasn't frivolous. He had a history of mental illness. He had been diagnosed as having a schizoid personality disorder and had been institutionalized for several years. While in police custody, Hill was consistently violent, throwing food and other objects through his cell bars, shouting obscenities at guards, trashing his cell, and ripping out his toilet bowl and smashing it against the bars of his cell.

His assigned lawyer was one of the more experienced attorneys on a list of attorneys assigned to represent indigent defendants. She was able to relate to him on a personal level and managed to keep him relatively subdued. She actually didn't think he was crazy, just filled with rage that he was being prosecuted, but she pursued vigorously his insanity defense.

The victims all gave powerful testimony. The defense didn't call a psychiatric expert. It sought instead to demonstrate through cross-examining the women that the defendant behaved so erratically and irrationally that he clearly must have been of unsound mind. His lawyer showed that he committed the crimes in the middle of the day when customers would most likely be present; Hill did not force the women to lock the stores; he left the "Open" sign prominently displayed on the front door; and his comments to the women were incoherent gibberish. I called Dr. Alan Furst, a highly respected psychiatrist who testified that in his opinion Hill behaved rationally, was well aware of his actions, and understood that his conduct was unlawful.

The defense lawyer in cross-examining Dr. Furst tried to reinforce Hill's mental and emotional instability by pointing to Hill's violent conduct in jail. On redirect examination, I asked Dr. Furst if, in his opinion, Hill's violence was a subterfuge. His answer: "No, it's not a subterfuge. He is the most violent person I have ever encountered. He's angry, very angry. But he's not crazy." Needless to say, the impact of that answer was devastating. Hill was convicted and sentenced to 200 years in prison (eight rapes times twenty-five years, the maximum punishment for rape).

All of this leads up to another story. During a lunch break during the Hill trial, after Dr. Furst testified, the detective who investigated the case and was my liaison with the witnesses and the police (we will call him Dan) stared at me, started to cry, and said he wanted to kill himself. Stunned, my first response was to ask him for his gun, which he gave me. After summoning one of my investigators to my office, I called Dr. Furst and asked him to come to my office immediately. He talked to Dan privately. I called Dan's commanding officer and Dan's wife and they both arrived shortly. Dan's wife was an attractive woman who looked drained and scared. She took Dan home.

The next time I saw Dan was a few years later in Brooklyn's Supreme Court building where I was trying a case for the special prosecutor's office. Dan was seated on a bench outside one of the courtrooms. I said hello, not knowing at the time why he was there. I assumed he was involved in a court case. I found out later that he was in the courthouse as a defendant in his own case. He was on trial for murder, charged with shooting his wife to death. He raised the insanity defense and was acquitted by reason of insanity.

Several years later, while taking my children to the Thanksgiving Day parade, we were walking past one of the elegant buildings on Central Park West and I noticed the doorman. It was Dan. I didn't know what to say except "hello, how are you?" and then I walked away.

A prosecutor's world is surrounded by crime, victims, tragedy, and sometimes strange and uncanny events. Sadness, fear, pain, and hope are always close. The experiences are often unpredictable, and sometimes unforgettable.

The Jury as "Conscience of the Community"

The jury has been hailed as one of the greatest attributes of our democracy. The jury has been called the "conscience of the community." Jury service gives ordinary citizens the opportunity to participate in the administration of justice. Acting in secrecy and without legal accountability for its decisions, the jury acts as a bulwark to vindicate the rule of law and prevent governmental oppression.

A trial by jury is one of the most intellectually fascinating and stressful events a prosecutor can experience. The prosecutor controls the process. After the jury is selected, the prosecutor leads off with an opening argument to introduce the case, describes the evidence he or she will offer, and explains why the defendant will be proven guilty beyond a reasonable doubt. Studies of jury decision-making suggest that a powerful opening statement by the prosecutor almost always predisposes the jury to convict, even without their hearing any of the evidence. Prosecutors know that juries usually view them as "champions of justice," trust their judgment, and believe that the prosecutor would not bring a case to trial unless the prosecutor is confident that the defendant is guilty and has the evidence to prove it. Jurors are probably aware that innocent persons sometimes might be brought to trial and might be mistakenly convicted, but jurors also know that this is a risk in any trial and that a very high burden of proof is imposed on prosecutors and juries.

Jurors frequently wanted to chat with me after a verdict. Some jurors wanted to talk about the evidence, judge, and defense lawyer, and about what went on during deliberations. It was strange to talk so intimately to people I had been staring at for weeks, always trying to discern what they were thinking, what they felt about me and the case as the proof was unfolding, and how they reacted to my summing up the case. Sometimes my interactions with jurors was awkward, even troubling, especially when a juror might exclaim that he knew the defendant was guilty just by looking at him.

Sometimes, however, jurors showed remarkable insight. I recall one case where the defendant was tried for the attempted murder of a police officer. After being spotted following an apartment burglary, the defendant fled down a flight of stairs pursued by several police officers. During the flight, the defendant turned and fired a gun at an officer, missed, was apprehended, and arrested. One of the key issues at trial was whether or not the defendant raised his arm to fire the gun or whether the gun he was holding in his hand went off accidentally. The evidence from witnesses went both ways and the jury's resolution of that issue, needless to say, would be critical.

During its deliberations the jury asked for all of the exhibits, including the gun, which is standard practice. The deliberations lasted a little over a day, and they found the defendant guilty of attempted murder. After the conviction, we chatted. The jurors told me they had examined the gun carefully, and tried to pull the trigger. They discovered a key fact that I confessed to them I had overlooked. Pulling the trigger of the gun required considerable force. To the jury, this "experiment" decisively negated the defendant's claim that his gun discharged accidentally from his finger touching the trigger.

Another case I prosecuted produced a bizarre postscript about juries. Three defendants were charged with kidnapping a government informant (who was subsequently murdered) to prevent him from testifying the following week in a major federal drug case. They also kidnapped an acquaintance of his, Artemio H., who was with him in an Upper West Side bar when they were both abducted by the trio. The indictment charged two kidnappings, but my only witness was Artemio. He was a difficult witness. He had been hospitalized for serious mental disorders and was recently released. But what a compelling narrative he told! He was blindfolded and imprisoned in a secret underground crypt in Harlem—a complex maze of tunnels, hideaways, and byways. He somehow managed to undo his binds, climb up on a cabinet to reach an air-conditioning duct, shimmy through the narrow opening, and crawl several hundred feet to a walkway that opened onto the street. Given his disheveled, grimy, and frantic appearance, nobody stopped to help him. He managed to get home to his Upper West Side room.

As I prepared the case for trial, a key fact that I believed confirmed Artemio's bizarre account was his story of how he had fled in terror by climbing out of his window and onto the fire escape when he heard someone bang on his door. It was a police officer looking for him, but Artemio told me he thought it was one of his kidnappers returning to kill him. Photos taken by investigators of the dungeon-like crypt were introduced into evidence.

The jury deliberated over four days without reaching a verdict. They asked the judge several times to repeat his instructions on reasonable doubt. Late at night on the fifth day of deliberations, the jury sent a note to the judge that went something like this: "Can we find that only one of the persons was kidnapped even though the indictment charges that both persons were abducted together?" The jury obviously was trying to negotiate a compromise. It was clear at that moment to everybody in the courtroom that the jury wanted to convict the defendants for at least one of the kidnappings. Nobody left the courtroom, recognizing that a split verdict would be arriving soon. It did. Guilty for kidnapping Artemio; not guilty for kidnapping the informant.

The next morning, the officer at the desk in the lobby alerted me that somebody wanted to see me. I recognized the name. It was the foreman of the jury. He smiled and we shook hands. He wanted to explain to me what had happened. He described in great detail the course of the lengthy deliberations, the hang-ups, the angry interchanges, the steadfast "reasonable doubt" jurors, and the dynamics on that final day and evening when the leaders of the two factions (the foreman led the "guilty on all counts" faction—his opposing juror led the "Not Guilty" faction) stood next to each other in the jury room looking out a window and speculating on how much longer the judge would keep them sequestered to force them to continue to deliberate. The judge had already given the jury the so-called "dynamite" instruction, which effectively tries to blast a verdict by emphasizing the need to return a verdict if at all possible. The two leaders decided to negotiate a compromise; guilt for kidnapping Artemio H., and not guilty for kidnapping the absent informant. They consulted their constituencies. The verdict sheet was signed. The courtroom was silent and tense as the foreman read the verdict. The jury was polled, and all agreed on the verdict.

Jurors do compromise. That's not just theory. Looking back, I wish the foreman had not told me what happened. I would have preferred the uncertainty of not knowing how my jury decided the case. The jury system does not operate in an ideal fashion when a verdict is based on a negotiated settlement, even if it does result in a guilty defendant getting convicted and punished. Although I know juries do it, it diminishes the jury's majestic role as the "conscience of the community," undermines the integrity of the trial, and gives a prosecutor a dubious victory.

Exploiting Courtroom Technology

Prosecutors increasingly use technology in the courtroom to win convictions. Sometimes technology is used responsibly, but sometimes it isn't. One of the most inflammatory techniques to get juries to convict is a prosecutor's use of a PowerPoint presentation during the closing argument to visually depict images of the crime emblazoned with the prosecutor's inflammatory captions. The prosecutor expects that the jury will react to these graphic images with grief, anger, and vengeance. As with the introduction of gruesome photographs, prosecutors are able to generate emotionally driven responses, sometimes without the juror even being aware that this is happening, and through this improper technique, to prejudice the decision-making process. Although there is nothing inherently wrong with using technology in the courtroom, more and more prosecutors cross the line by exploiting the power of technology to distort the way that juries analyze the evidence and thereby impair a defendant's right to a fair trial.

Examples abound: A prosecutor summed up in a murder trial arising from a gang shootout by using a sixty-seven-slide PowerPoint presentation, in full color, which included images of the victim's bloody body emblazoned in bright red lettering with the words MURDER, TERROR, and FEAR; another referred to the victims as HELPLESS; and another prominently displayed his pronouncement: THE DEFENDANT IS GUILTY OF ALL THE CHARGES AGAINST HIM. Prosecutors have superimposed the words DEFENDANT GUILTY OF PREMEDITATED MURDER over an image of the victim's bloody body, and the words GUILTY BEYOND A REASONABLE DOUBT over the defendant's booking photo. Prosecutors have displayed slides with images of a gun and red circles that resemble pools of blood. Another prosecutor used slides showing the defendant's booking photographs with captions DO YOU BELIEVE HIM? and WHY SHOULD YOU BELIEVE ANYTHING HE SAYS? Another prosecutor showed slides of the defendant's mug shot with the word GUILTY superimposed diagonally in red letters in opposite directions forming an X shape across the defendant's face.

In addition to prosecutors using technology creatively to impress the jury with inflammatory images, prosecutors also use technology to influence juries with visual trickery.

One creative ploy is to distort the jury's understanding of the concept of reasonable doubt. Prosecutors have used a PowerPoint program with a slide show containing several pieces in a puzzle which they show to the jury on the screen sequentially, but they omit a few pieces. The image from the pieces that are shown is immediately recognizable—for example, a picture of the Statue of Liberty, or a well-known celebrity. The slide show finishes before the last pieces are in place; a few pieces of the puzzle are missing. In the Statue of Liberty puzzle, for example, the prosecutor leaves out the piece in the center, which includes a portion of the statue's face, and another piece in the upper corner of the image which shows a portion of the torch. In presenting this slide show, the prosecutor tells the jury that they know what the picture is, beyond a reasonable doubt, even without having to see all the pieces of the puzzle.

The prosecutor's clever gambit dilutes the standard of proof necessary to convict. By using such an immediately recognizable iconic image, the prosecutor suggests to the jury that they don't really need all the pieces to decide what the picture is, just as they don't need to be certain of all the facts to know that the defendant is guilty beyond a reasonable doubt. Thus, the prosecutor leaves the jury with the impression that the standard of proof of beyond a reasonable doubt involves a similarly easy and quantitative analysis; pieces can be left out but the jury still knows the result.

Many psychological studies confirm that visual arguments have a unique power to manipulate audiences by exploiting conscious and unconscious emotional and reasoning processes, and the impact of visual devices on jury decision-making is well-recognized. Moreover, and most critically, visual manipulations of the sort used by prosecutors in the above cases are inconsistent with the fundamental principle of a fair criminal justice system that embodies reasoned analyses and careful deliberation. This is not to say that prosecutors should not use technology and visual aids to promote effective advocacy. Courts should be willing to permit advocacy techniques that assist the jury's understanding of the evidence and encourage the jury to engage in responsible fact-finding. However, technology is misused when it is done to dazzle, mislead, confuse, and impede the search for truth. A jury's deliberations must be based exclusively on the evidence and the law, and not on the ability of a prosecutor by an emotionally persuasive kaleidoscopic experience to manipulate and distort the evidence and thereby undermine the integrity of the trial.

Subverting the "Golden Rule"

Prosecutors, as all lawyers, often engage in over-the-top oratory. They love to play to the jury, and jurors typically eat it up. Inflammatory rhetoric commonly hits the mark, but prosecutors have to be more careful than other lawyers. A private lawyer's goal is to represent a client competently and ethically. A prosecutor's goal is to do justice.

Some prosecutors revel in name-calling and character assassination. They refer to defendants as "worms," "germs," "trash," "rats," "animals," "mad dogs," "subhuman," "rancid," and "rotten." They align defendants with infamous villains such as Hitler, Saddam Hussein, Charles Manson, Jeffrey Dahmer. They exploit the jury's sympathy for the victim to incite feelings of rage and revenge. Prosecutors demand that juries pay the defendant back. They exhort the jury to listen to the victim lying in her grave crying out to the jury to "Avenge Me, Avenge Me." Some of this inflammatory conduct could be dark comedy if the stakes weren't so high.

A favorite trick of prosecutors is to invoke the "Golden Rule." The Golden Rule is an ethical precept from the New Testament (Matthew, Luke) that counsels persons to do unto others as you would have them do unto you. The typical jury argument in criminal cases is to ask jurors to imagine themselves in the place of the victim and to wreak vengeance against the defendant for what he did to the victim. This argument is universally condemned because it encourages jurors to abandon impartiality and objectivity and decide the case on the basis of personal feelings of prejudice, bias, and revenge. Prosecutors are aware of the prohibition of this kind of argument but they also know that it works.

A relatively recent variation of the Golden Rule argument is called "channeling." It is a rhetorical device used in murder cases in which a prosecutor transforms himself or herself into the body, mind, and voice of the victim, and speaks to the jury in the first person as though the victim were speaking. The prosecutor narrates the victim's thoughts, fears, and anguish at the moment the victim is confronted and killed by the defendant. The prosecutor recreates the terror felt by the victim as the prosecutor relates the horrific moments just before the victim is killed. Needless to say, given the almost unendurable ending, and the experience of death recreated, a prosecutor's channeling can be an incredibly powerful technique to bring the vivid moments just before the victim's death into the courtroom and inflame the jury with incalculable prejudice.

In a recent murder case, the defendant concededly killed the victim with a shotgun blast but claimed the victim forcibly entered his home without invitation and was killed by the defendant in self-defense. The prosecutor's closing argument assumed the identity of the victim: "My name is Alan. I was fifty-five years old when I was ambushed and murdered by the Defendant." The prosecutor describes the events leading up to the shooting in the voice of Alan. "I see Mark raise a shotgun, this twelve-gauge shotgun. I look at Mark. I'm scared. I say to him, 'Mark, please don't shoot.' I didn't stop him. He fired one single twelve-gauge round directly into my belly. I fall backwards."

Again, in the victim's voice, the prosecutor goes on to narrate the events after the shooting, describing the police arriving and the victim dying: "I can hear sirens arriving. I'm still barely alive, but not really conscious. The deputy eventually comes up to my near lifeless body. He calls 'Flight for Life.' A few minutes later the helicopter lands and the medical staff and the police get me into the helicopter, take me to the hospital. Somewhere between that flight from the defendant's residence to the hospital, I die." The defendant was found guilty.

Did the prosecutor's gambit violate the defendant's right to a fair trial? An appeals court thought so and reversed the conviction. As the court noted, a jury trial is not an unregulated slugfest in which the combatants can inflict foul blows at will. There are rules of engagement that all lawyers are supposed to follow, especially prosecutors who, given their power and prestige with juries, probably wield more influence and persuasive power in a courtroom than any other lawyer. Although all lawyers violate the rules on occasion, prosecutors seem to violate the rules most often and with impunity, and often without any significant oversight or accountability.

The prosecutor's channeling narrative also violates rules barring a prosecutor from expressing personal opinions about the evidence, including what the prosecutor imagines are the victim's thoughts and feelings before he died—describing the victim as "scared" and "surprised." The prosecutor thereby manipulates the evidence to include his or her own opinion of what the victim might have testified to, but did not, and certainly with no opportunity for the defendant to cross-examine the fictitious witness created by the prosecutor.

As with all lawyers, prosecutors want to win but they have a special duty to serve justice. They are allowed to win fairly and not by using unethical tricks.

Junk Science in the Courtroom

Prosecutors often use scientific evidence to get convictions. Prosecutors can use scientific evidence responsibly, but they also can manipulate scientific evidence to get convictions, sometimes when the defendant is actually innocent.

One of the most famous examples of a prosecutor's misuse of scientific evidence is *Miller v. Pate*, a prosecution for the brutal sexual attack and murder of an eight-year-old girl. The prosecutor introduced into evidence a pair of men's undershorts allegedly worn by the defendant which were found near the crime scene, and which the prosecutor claimed were stained by the victim's blood. The prosecutor called a chemist from the state's crime laboratory who testified that the blood type on the shorts matched the victim's blood. In summation, the prosecutor repeatedly told the jury that the scientific evidence connecting the defendant's "bloody shorts" to the victim irrefutably proved his guilt. The defendant was convicted and sentenced to death.

However, the stains on the shorts were not blood but paint. At a hearing ten years later, a new scientific expert confirmed this, and there was testimony that the trial prosecutor knew this but continued to misrepresent the shorts as "a garment heavily stained with blood." The conviction was vacated.

Miller v. Pate is not an isolated example. The records of contemporary criminal trials are replete with instances of prosecutors using false and erroneous opinions by experts, as well as the use of unsupported "junk science," to win convictions. Prosecutors know that juries rely heavily on scientific experts as possessing a special aura of reliability, even infallibility. Some experts used by prosecutors have become infamous for their baseless opinions. Dozens of convictions have been reversed based on the erroneous opinions of prosecution experts: Fred Zain, a West Virginia serologist who had a long history of falsifying evidence; Joyce Gilchrist, an Oklahoma City serologist who systematically gave false testimony; Arnold Melnikoff, director of Montana's crime laboratory who gave hair comparison testimony that was repeatedly debunked by peer groups as being without any scientific basis; Louise Robbins, a California foot-comparison expert whose opinions were ridiculed by courts and peer groups as "junk science."

Melnikoff's opinions of hair comparisons are noteworthy. Although hair comparison is recognized as one of the weakest types of forensic evidence, Melnikoff typically gave opinions that hair found at a crime scene was indistinguishable from those of the defendant. He would make up astronomical statistics supposedly to establish that the chances of the hair being from someone other than the defendant were more than 1 in 10,000. His statistics, as any responsible prosecutor should have known, were without any scientific basis. The conviction of the defendants in the notorious "Central Park Jogger" case in which the defendants were later exonerated featured the prosecutor's use of an expert's hair comparison testimony in which the expert testified that hair found on the victim was "consistent" with the hair of one of the defendants. In her summation the prosecutor misrepresented the testimony of the expert, arguing that the expert concluded there was a "perfect match" between hair found on the victim and the hair of the defendants.

The advent of DNA evidence has exposed much of this fake science. In a New York exoneration, the defendant, Roy Brown, was convicted of murder based largely on an expert's testimony that a bite mark on the victim's arm matched the defendant. This opinion was erroneous, as DNA evidence would later reveal. A 2009 report by the National Academy of Sciences presents a scathing critique of several types of forensic evidence, including hair, bullet fragments, and bite mark testimony. The report concludes that experts cannot consistently agree on whether an injury is a human bite mark and cannot identify the source of the bite mark with reasonable accuracy. Prosecutors are acutely aware of the shortcomings of forensic science, but routinely seek out experts who will give them the opinion they want, regardless of its reliability, and prosecutors reject experts who display independence and refuse to give the prosecutor the opinion he or she wants.

That is exactly what happened in the Brown case. As revealed at a posttrial hearing, the prosecutor had asked one of the nation's leading forensic odontologists to analyze the bite marks on the victim's body. The expert "excluded" Brown as the source of the bite marks. This opinion was not all that surprising. Brown had only four teeth while the bite marks on the victim's body showed six teeth. The prosecutor did not call this expert, instructed the expert not to write down his opinion, and did not disclose his opinion to the defense. The prosecutor then found another expert who gave the prosecutor the opinion he wanted. And the prosecutor, along with his expert, explained to the jury that the extra teeth marks were the result of a struggle during the attack.

The former district attorney of Oklahoma City stated: "An expert who won't give you the opinion you want in not a whole lot of value to you." So, instead of seeking good science and the truth, some prosecutors are willing to settle for poor science and something less than the truth. One would think that prosecutors sworn to serve justice would be leading the movement toward protecting the integrity of the fact-finding process from fraudulent and erroneous scientific evidence, not promoting fraudulent testimony by experts. Prosecutors should be working to improve the quality and independence of scientific and forensic laboratories, many of which are still in the control of police agencies that work with the prosecutor. Prosecutors should be vigilant to scrutinize carefully opinions from experts that lack a valid scientific basis.

Prosecutors and Race

One would think that prosecutors, as ministers of justice, would be colorblind when it comes to race. But sadly, the history of U.S. prosecution suggests otherwise. Prosecutors have incited juries to substitute racial stereotypes for evidence and racial prejudice for reason. Prosecutors often tried to inflame a jury's racial fears and stereotypes with predictions of bloodshed, terror, and violence unless the jury convicted the accused black man. Where this has occurred, the arguments are not subtle. They include: "Unless you hang this Negro, white people won't be safe"; "How would you like to have your daughter on a train with nine Negroes in a car"; "I am well enough acquainted with this class of niggers to know that they have got it in for the white race in their heart"; "It will not be safe if you permit a Negro to come in and slaughter a white man"; "You should consider the fact that Mary Sue Rowe is a young white woman and that this defendant is a black man for the purpose of determining his intent at the time he entered Mrs. Rowe's home"; "The defendant is a big, black gorilla with arms as long as your legs"; "The jury should deal harshly with such cattle."

Arguably, such blatant appeals to racial prejudice by prosecutors may have been isolated examples, and they occur much less frequently today. When they do, a conviction usually is reversed, but not always. Indeed, the U.S. Supreme Court recently refused to review a narcotics conviction in which the prosecutor ridiculed the defendant's innocent explanation that he did not know that other persons in a hotel room were involved in a drug deal with the following sarcastic question:

> You've got African-Americans, you've got Hispanics, you've got a bag full of money. Does that tell you—a light bulb doesn't go off in your head and say, This is a drug deal?

Because the defense lawyer inexplicably did not object to the prosecutor's racially charged insinuation, the appellate court did not overturn the conviction. And because of the defense lawyer's failure, the Supreme Court did not grant review. Nevertheless, Justice Sotomayor, joined by Justice Breyer, wrote a separate opinion to make it absolutely clear that the court's denial of review did not indicate tolerance for the prosecutor's pernicious remark. "By suggesting that race should play a role in establishing a defendant's criminal intent," Justice Sotomayor wrote, "the prosecutor here tapped a deep and sorry vein of racial prejudice that has run through the history of criminal justice in our nation. By arousing the jury's deep-seated prejudice, the prosecutor sought to persuade the jury to convict the defendant not because he was guilty but because he was black."

The prosecutor's remark was bad enough. Equally bad was the response from the prosecutor's office that handled the appeal. Its brief characterized the prosecutor's question as "impolitic" and argued that the defendant was not prejudiced by the prosecutor's remark, "even assuming the question crossed the line." Given the way the prosecutor's conduct was marginalized by his own office, it is not surprising that no disciplinary action was taken even though the prosecutor, in making the racially charged comment, violated the rules of professional ethics.

Race has also played a dominant role in death penalty trials. Operating on the assumption that the race of the victim is a silent aggravating factor in a jury's determination to impose the death penalty, prosecutors have used the race of the victim in deciding whether to charge murder as a capital crime. The statistics are shocking: in many states, defendants charged with killing white victims have been at least four times, and as much as eight times, more likely to be charged with capital murder and receive a death sentence as those defendants charged with killing black victims in otherwise similar cases. A famous study—the "Baldus Study"—examined over 2,000 murder cases in Georgia and isolated 230 nonracial variables. The study concluded that the odds of a defendant receiving a death sentence were 4.3 times greater if the victim was white than if the victim was black. Other studies have found even higher disparities.

Despite this clear documentation of a prosecutor's use of race to charge a defendant with capital murder, the Supreme

Court in *McCleskey v. Kemp* did not find that the prosecutor engaged in unconstitutional discrimination. McCleskey has been called the "Dred Scott" decision of the twentieth century. In one of his greatest dissents, Justice William Brennan wrote that "the way [prosecutors] choose those who will die reveals the depth of moral commitment among the living."

Warren McCleskey was not the actual killer of the white victim but the killer's accomplice. The actual killer made a deal with the prosecutor and testified against him. McCleskey was executed on September 25, 1991.

Finally, race often plays an important role in a prosecutor's selection of the jury. Prosecutors, as well as defense lawyers, historically were free to remove every black person from a jury without needing to give any reason. Then, in 1986, in the case of *Batson v. Kentucky*, the Supreme Court declared that striking jurors because of their race is unconstitutional. The court also held, however, that prosecutors were free to strike black jurors if they could give a race-neutral reason for doing so. Prosecutors thereafter became adept at concocting far-fetched but "race-neutral" reasons for their strikes, such as that the juror "seemed inattentive," "didn't seem sincere," "was overeducated," "was undereducated." Even a prosecutor striking a juror based on a "hunch," or a "gut feeling," was an acceptable reason. It should therefore come as no surprise that in many states prosecutors strike black jurors far more often than white jurors.

In a blatant scheme to get rid of black jurors, prosecutors compiled lists of potential jurors that highlighted the names of the jurors who were black and kept a series of notes from an investigator as to which of these jurors would be the most acceptable. Astonishingly, the prosecutors actually claimed that striking these jurors was for reasons other than race. The Supreme Court, in vacating the defendant's conviction because of the prosecutor's conduct, found the prosecutor's claim of race-neutral strikes "nonsense." The court described how the prosecutor accepted white jurors for giving the same answers to questions that were the basis for striking the black jurors.

Why do prosecutors seek to keep black people from serving as jurors? The answer is obvious. Prosecutors have long believed that striking black jurors improves their chances of convicting a black defendant. Prosecutors assume that black people are more likely than white people to have negative feelings about government, to have had bad experiences with the police, are more likely to have been targeted for arrests and forcible stops than white people, are more likely to have been imprisoned for minor drug crimes, and are more likely to believe that crimes against black victims are prosecuted less aggressively than crimes against whites. Certainly some black jurors, like some white jurors, may feel this way, and they can be dismissed accordingly, but they cannot be dismissed simply because of their race.

Prosecutors have been trained on how to evade the Batson rule. In a training video leaked from the Philadelphia

District Attorney's Office, new prosecutors were told that when they encountered black jurors to "mark something down on a little sheet that you can articulate later" and "to ask more questions of those people [black jurors] so it gives you more ammunition to make an articulable reason as to why you are striking them not for race." North Carolina prosecutors held training sessions with handouts for "Batson Justifications: Articulating Juror Negatives," which listed a variety of reasons for striking black jurors based on the kinds of pretextual reasons noted above.

Although race continues to be a factor in prosecution decisions such as bail, charging, jury selection, and sentencing, there may be reason to be hopeful that the times are changing. African-Americans are slowly but surely winning elections for local district attorney, and there appears to be increased attention by lawmakers and courts as to how prosecutor decisions impact racial equality in the criminal justice system.

Chapter Four

Florida v. George Zimmerman: The Killing of Trayvon Martin

Background

The fatal shooting of Trayvon Martin by George Zimmerman on February 26, 2012, in Sanford, Florida, ignited a firestorm of controversy and exposed the bitter racial divide in America. Even President Obama weighed in, commenting: "This could have been my son"; "Trayvon Martin could have been me 35 years ago."

Martin, a seventeen-year-old African-American, was shot to death by Zimmerman, the neighborhood watch commander at the gated townhouse community where Martin was staying with his father's fiancé. Zimmerman claimed that Martin was behaving "suspiciously," and alerted the police in a recorded conversation in which he stated: "He looks black," "I don't know what his deal is," and "these assholes, they always get away." After the police told Zimmerman they would respond and not to get involved, Zimmerman claimed that Martin confronted him and they struggled violently. Witnesses gave different accounts of the fight. Zimmerman, whose head appeared to be cut, and his nose bleeding, claimed that Martin jumped on top of him and started beating him, that he called for help repeatedly, and then in fear for his life, shot Martin.

Zimmerman was detained by the police for questioning. He passed a voice stress test to see if he was lying. After five hours he was released. The police said there was no evidence to refute Zimmerman's claim that he acted in self-defense, and under Florida's "Stand Your Ground" law, the police could not make a lawful arrest.

After widespread protests over the police department's refusal to arrest Zimmerman, the police turned the case over to the Seminole County Attorney's Office for review, which immediately announced that a grand jury would be convened to investigate the shooting. However, given the uproar over the way the case had been handled, Florida's governor appointed State Attorney Angela Corey as a special prosecutor to investigate the case. Corey announced that her office would decide on its own whether to bring charges, and would not present the case to a grand jury. As she stated: "I always lean toward moving forward without needing the grand jury in a case like this. I foresee us being able to make a decision. And move on it on our own." Corey's office ultimately charged Zimmerman with second-degree murder.

The trial of *State v. Zimmerman* began on June 10, 2013, with the selection of a six-person jury. Six women were selected to serve as jurors; five were white and one was non-white. The trial lasted a month.

Why Did Special Prosecutor Corey Bypass the Grand Jury?

Special prosecutor Corey brought a formal complaint charging Zimmerman with second-degree murder. The complaint was based on a hearsay affidavit filed by her office explaining the factual basis for the charge. From the outset there was a huge question whether under any version of the facts Zimmerman actually committed the crime of murder, or a lesser degree of homicide such as manslaughter, or, indeed, whether he committed any crime at all. Since Zimmerman did not plead guilty, the affidavit by itself, which summarized the investigation by the special prosecutor's office, required Zimmerman to stand trial without a grand jury having heard any evidence and voting to indict him. He was charged with murder simply on the hearsay statements of two investigators who summarized their versions of the evidence they learned from witnesses, as well as other forensic evidence. The special prosecutor, in effect, was a one person grand jury, and a hardly neutral one at that.

This procedure appears troubling, even improper. As discussed in Chapter 2, the grand jury is the principal charging instrument in our criminal justice system. Is a prosecutor allowed to bypass the grand jury and bring charges on his or her own? The grand jury was established long ago as a shield against oppressive prosecutions. The Magna Carta amplified the grand jury's role as a buffer against the uncontrolled power of the King. The grand jury traditionally has served to protect an individual from false accusations except by "the lawful judgment of his peers," and is explicitly provided for in the Fifth Amendment to the U.S. Constitution. If that is so, was Corey allowed to bypass the grand jury and charge Zimmerman all by herself with murder? The answer is straightforward. In 1884, the Supreme Court in *Hurtado v. California* explicitly held that the Constitution does not require states to use grand juries to formally charge crimes; only the federal government is required to do so.

Of course, states have the power to require grand juries to bring indictments, and most states do, but not Florida. Unless the charge is murder in the first degree—a "capital" murder—no grand jury is required. Zimmerman was not charged with capital murder. That is the reason Florida used a grand jury in the celebrated 2011 trial of Casey Anthony for murdering her little boy; she was charged with capital murder. Still, under Florida law, Corey could have asked a grand jury to hear the evidence in the Zimmerman case and return an indictment. Why did she not do this?

One plausible reason might be contained in the Florida Grand Jury handbook, distributed to grand jurors when they are empaneled. It states:

> Except for capital crimes, the state attorney (or statewide prosecutor) may initiate all other charges. The grand jury of course may indict for any crime that the evidence justifies.

The wisdom of leaving to the state attorney's discretion (or the statewide prosecutor) the bringing of all charges less than capital murder charges is readily apparent. If a grand jury was required to initiate the prosecution of less serious crimes—even minor offenses like traffic infractions—the grand jury would be so overburdened with accusations that it might not be able to perform its more important duties.

So how do all the other states manage? Many states such as New York require that grand juries must indict defendants on all felony charges absent a waiver by the defendant, which rarely happens. The New York grand jury system appears to be working effectively. The Florida handbook, however, justifies the avoidance of grand juries in order to save the grand jury system from the needless time and expense of having to review ordinary run-of-the-mill offenses. However, a charge of murder in the second degree is hardly a "run-of-the-mill" offense, especially since a conviction could result in a sentence of life imprisonment.

Still, given the high-profile nature of the case, should not Corey have presented the case to the grand jury? One can only speculate on her reasons. It is conceivable that Corey was concerned that the grand jury might become a so-called "runaway jury," that is, a grand jury that might have been so offended by Zimmerman's conduct that it might have insisted on indicting him for first-degree capital murder, which requires the element of premeditation, which Corey apparently believed she would not be able to sustain at a trial. Or, perhaps more likely, Corey may have been concerned that the local grand jury in Seminole County might have been composed of pro-Zimmerman, or "Stand Your Ground" partisans, who might have decided not to indict at all, believing that the encounter was ratcheted up to a frenetic pitch by outside "agitators" and "race baiters." The grand jurors may have believed there was no racial animus on Zimmerman's part, and that his motivation was to protect the safety of the community and himself from a dangerous person. It is interesting that Corey's affidavit described a "struggle" between Zimmerman and Martin, but there was no other reference to self-defense or the controversial "stand your ground" claim that Zimmerman had argued, and the police originally accepted, as the justification for shooting Martin.

Of course it is conceivable that Corey was concerned that the case was weak and would be difficult to prove at trial beyond a reasonable doubt. She may have wanted to avoid making her task at trial even more difficult by having witnesses give testimony in a grand jury and thereby lock themselves into their versions of the events. If they then gave a different version at trial, they would be subject to attack by a skilled defense attorney who would be able to show that their inconsistent versions made their testimony unworthy of belief. Perhaps Corey may have wanted to avoid the claim that her critics might have pressed: that her presentation of the evidence in the grand jury was skewed, and that she failed to present evidence that might have exonerated Zimmerman.

A possible clue to Corey's decision may have emerged at Zimmerman's bail hearing when his attorney asked a key investigator in the case whether he knew who started the fight, and whether he had any evidence to contradict the fact that Martin punched Zimmerman first and then banged his head onto the concrete. To both questions the investigator answered "No." The evidence, in other words, may have originally appeared so equivocal that Corey did not want to risk its early disclosure.

There is no doubt that a prosecutor's decision to avoid using a grand jury for any of these reasons could be viewed as the action of a prudent prosecutor, especially when Florida's grand jury statute clearly affords a prosecutor that option. In fact, most prosecutors, if they are candid, probably would acknowledge that since they ultimately have to try the case, and want to convict a defendant they believe to be guilty, the most strategically sound pretrial decision would be to put the prosecutor's case in the most winnable posture and avoid making unnecessary mistakes in the grand jury.

Nevertheless, is circumventing the grand jury the proper course to take? Given the massive publicity surrounding such a sensational case—it rivaled the intensity of the racial firestorm surrounding the O.J. Simpson trial—circumventing the grand jury was risky. Deciding to use Florida's escape hatch to forego a procedure designed to protect a defendant's liberty from unwarranted accusations appears inconsistent with a prosecutor's mission to serve the cause of justice. This is not to suggest that George Zimmerman deserves more justice than anyone else in Florida who probably would also not be indicted by a grand jury, but it is puzzling why a procedure so ingrained in U.S. law and culture as a protection of an accused may be so easily ignored. If a prosecutor chooses not to present this type of case to a grand jury so that the grand jury might, as the Florida handbook states, perform its "important duties," what exactly are those important duties except to provide a measure of protection for an accused and against the government?

Did the Special Prosecutor Overcharge Zimmerman?

After the first week of testimony in the Zimmerman trial it became clear that Special Prosecutor Corey may have overcharged Zimmerman with murder in the second degree, which raises some interesting questions. Do prosecutors typically overcharge defendants? Why would a prosecutor decide to bring more serious charges that the prosecutor may believe cannot be sustained by the evidence? Is it ethical for a prosecutor to bring charges that the prosecutor believes cannot reasonably be supported by the evidence?

Anyone who follows criminal law closely knows that a prosecutor's charging decision, as explained in Chapter 1, is the crux of the prosecutor's function. Charging crimes involves the most awesome use of a prosecutor's power, and is virtually unreviewable by courts. As noted often in this book, a prosecutor's decision to bring charges probably is the most dangerous aspect of the prosecutor's function, and often invites abuse.

George Zimmerman admitted from the outset that he killed Trayvon Martin. Special Prosecutor Corey had the discretion to select the charge from three homicide statutes—first-degree murder, second-degree murder, and manslaughter. And she could have declined to bring any charges. Under Florida law, first-degree murder requires a killing with a "premeditated design," and is a capital offense. Second-degree murder requires proof that the killer acted with a "depraved mind" but without premeditation. Manslaughter requires proof that the killer acted with "culpable negligence" and "without lawful justification."

A first-degree murder charge was never a plausible option because there was no proof that Zimmerman had a preconceived plan to cause Martin's death. But was there sufficient proof that would support a charge of second-degree murder, namely, that in causing Martin's death Zimmerman acted with a "depraved mind?" At the time that Corey filed her probable cause affidavit was there a reasonable view of the evidence to support the allegation that Zimmerman in shooting Martin acted with a depraved mind? Even assuming the truth of the assertions in the affidavit that Zimmerman "profiled" Martin, "followed" him, "confronted" him, and engaged him in a "struggle" before shooting him, is there any reasonable theory from these assertions that would show that Zimmerman acted with a "depraved mind?" It is a significant stretch from these assertions to draw that conclusion. At most, his killing may have been committed, as manslaughter requires, with "culpable negligence" and without "lawful justification." But depraved mind murder?

Indeed, the first week's testimony supported the defense theory that Zimmerman may have been legally justified in using deadly force to defend himself. One prosecution witness testified that he heard people "running" and saw two people engaged in a struggle and "flailing their arms." Another witness testified that she saw two people struggling in a "ground and pound" encounter in which Martin appeared to be on top of Zimmerman. Photographs depicted Zimmerman's injuries—a bloody nose, scrapes, lumps, and two bloody cuts to his head. Evidence also was presented that showed that Zimmerman's clothes were wet in the back, containing bits of grass.

Whatever a jury makes of this evidence, it seems that under no reasonable view of the evidence could a prosecutor argue that Zimmerman acted with a "depraved mind." Why is this so? Because the concept of a depraved mind in criminal law traditionally is limited to cases in which a person may not necessarily intend to kill anyone but acts with a "wicked heart," and engages in conduct so wanton and heinous as to manifest an utter disregard for human life. The kinds of killings that historically have supported a theory of depraved mind murder involve cases like shooting into a crowd of people, planting a bomb in a public place, violently hitting a young child repeatedly, and driving a car at an excessive speed into a crowded thoroughfare.

Even assuming that in these examples the actor did not specifically intend to kill any particular person, it is inescapable that he had to have known that his conduct would almost certainly cause someone's death. Such depraved conduct therefore should be considered the equivalent of intentional murder. But bringing a charge of depraved mind murder when a death results from a violent physical encounter as in the Zimmerman–Martin encounter appears to be an unreasonable exercise of the prosecutor's charging power.

Why did Corey overcharge Zimmerman, knowing that the proof would support at most a conviction for manslaughter? One reason might have been to give her considerably more leverage in the event the defense was interested in pleading guilty. Some prosecutors do in fact bring more charges than the evidence realistically warrants, or higher degrees of charges than the evidence realistically warrants. They do this in the belief that a defendant faced with a choice between going to trial and being found guilty of the more serious charge might feel compelled to plead guilty to some lesser crime, and receive a lesser punishment. The defendant does not know what proof the prosecutor has to convict him or her. And so the pressure to go to trial may pose too great a risk for a defendant, even a defendant who is innocent. And prosecutors know that over 95 percent of defendants plead guilty. So overcharging as a coercive tactic to induce a guilty plea usually works.

Moreover, overcharging may work as a trial tactic as well. Overcharging can be a win-win proposition for a prosecutor at trial. Presumably a jury could decide to convict of the higher charge, however unreasonable such a decision might be, especially when the crime involves an unlawful killing. A jury's sympathy almost always goes to the victim. Also, every prosecutor knows that overcharging gives a jury the chance to compromise between higher and lesser counts. A jury verdict based on such a compromise would allow each member of the jury to feel that some measure of justice had been done.

Prosecutors, as a matter of professional ethics, are forbidden to file or maintain charges greater in number or degree than can reasonably be supported by the evidence. But the language of criminal statutes is often broad, vague, and subject to widely differing interpretations. Did Zimmerman kill martin with a wicked and wanton heart? Could a jury so find? Maybe.

The considerations that may have motivated Corey to charge Zimmerman with murder are unknown, but they may have included the enhanced leverage in the event Zimmerman sought a plea, and the opportunity for a jury to compromise between a greater and lesser degree of homicide. There may have been other considerations as well. Corey may have been influenced by public pressure to charge murder. Given the national and even international attention to the case, Corey's decision to bring a murder charge, whether or not reasonably based on the evidence, and whether or not motivated by personal or political considerations, appeared to have been a hugely popular decision. Since it was preliminary to the trial, and appeared at the time to be a responsible exercise of prosecutorial discretion, there was little criticism of her decision.

Whether Corey's decision to charge murder was a shrewd tactical maneuver to make a conviction more likely, or a tactical blunder that suggested her bad faith motivation to "pile on" a charge higher than the evidence reasonably warranted, is virtually impossible to know. Divining a prosecutor's actual motivation is always a hazardous quest. But as the Zimmerman trial continued, this quest yielded more concrete answers.

Sandbagging the Prosecution by Artificially Enhancing Zimmerman's Credibility

Sometimes prosecutors sandbag the defense. But sometimes prosecutors get sandbagged themselves. This happened early in the Zimmerman trial. During the cross-examination of Officer Chris Serino, a prosecution witness, Mark O'Mara, George Zimmerman's lawyer, asked Serino a highly improper question. After establishing from the witness that there were no significant discrepancies between

Zimmerman's description to the police of his encounter with Martin and the physical evidence and statements from neighbors, O'Mara asked Serino: "Do you think he was telling the truth?" Without any objection from the prosecution, Serino answered "Yes." The judge then recessed for the day.

The following morning, after hearing arguments from the prosecution, the judge instructed the jury to ignore Serino's remark that he believed Zimmerman was telling the truth. The judge's instruction to the jury to disregard Serino's comment was clearly correct. It is a well-established rule of courtroom testimony that a witness is forbidden from commenting on the credibility of another witness, or as in this case, the credibility of defendant Zimmerman. It is the exclusive province of the jury to make determinations of credibility, and a lawyer subverts that principle when he or she invites a witness to endorse the credibility of someone else. Indeed, convictions in child sexual abuse, domestic violence, rape, and drug prosecutions have been reversed when prosecutors have asked witnesses, typically expert witnesses, to give opinions that validate the truthfulness of a victim or a witness, or even give an opinion that a victim has in fact been abused.

The judge's instruction is familiar to persons who follow jury trials. Courts are committed to the theory that juries can ignore prejudicial evidence or improper conduct when properly instructed by the trial judge. Such "protective" or "curative" instructions advise the jurors to erase from their collective consciousness a prejudicial event that has occurred in the courtroom that might distort the jury's deliberations and verdict. Such instructions are commonly used when inadmissible evidence has been received, or prejudicial remarks are made by a lawyer, a witness, or even the judge, or when any other occurrence has happened at the trial that could impair the integrity of the proceedings. Of course, if the error or misconduct is serious enough, the judge could declare a mistrial.

But regardless of the theory behind such curative instructions, a bigger question is whether juries are actually capable of following such instructions. One is reminded of the courtroom moment in the classic film *Anatomy of a Murder* when the defense attorney, played by Jimmy Stewart, is cross-examining the prosecution's medical examiner in a murder case in which the defendant claimed the deceased had just raped his wife and that it was this event that triggered his killing him. After getting the doctor to admit that his autopsy of the deceased could have revealed that the deceased had recently ejaculated, thereby supporting the theory of the defense, Stewart then asks the witness, without any basis for asking the question, whether the witness was instructed by the prosecutor to conduct an examination "that would only be useful to the prosecution, but not to conduct an examination if it would be useful to the defense." The prosecutor jumps up and screams an objection and the judge, noting the clear impropriety of asking a baseless question, instructs the jury to disregard the question. As Stewart calmly returns to the counsel table, his associate smiles, and his client whispers, "How can a jury disregard something they've already heard?" Stewart answers, "They can't. They can't."

Instructing a jury to disregard something they've already heard has been assailed as a fiction, a judicial fraud, and is tantamount to telling a jury to "unring a bell." I typically ask students in my evidence class to "try not to think about a pink elephant." In fact, such instructions may be counterproductive because they call the jury's attention to something that it otherwise might have overlooked or forgotten, or, as in the Zimmerman case, gives added prominence to testimony that the jury heard the day before and had many hours to absorb.

Are juries capable and willing to follow such instructions? Or, to be more precise, is there a good chance that the Zimmerman jury followed the judge's instruction to disregard Officer Serino's testimony that he believed Zimmerman was telling the truth? Apart from our own intuition, psychological studies of jury decision-making suggest that jurors are not generally successful at ignoring information they have learned about, even when a judge instructs them to disregard that information. Although it is not a simple task to analyze the psychological factors that explain why a judge's instruction to a jury to disregard information is frequently unsuccessful, it is possible from the scientific literature to conclude that juror decision-making is influenced by attitudes and biases about crime, police, the justice system, and about the outcome of a case that they believe is fair and just.

Would the Zimmerman jury's verdict be influenced by Serino's improper testimony? Would the judge's instruction to the jury to disregard that testimony merely highlight it and compound the error? Or would the supposed fiction of a "curative instruction" actually work?

Were Prosecution Witnesses Coached to Give False and Misleading Testimony?

Four witnesses to the deadly encounter between Trayvon Martin and George Zimmerman gave statements to the police shortly after the occurrence that appeared to support Zimmerman's claim that he fatally shot Martin in self-defense. However, when these witnesses were reinterviewed by agents of Special State Prosecutor Corey several weeks later, they changed their stories in ways that weakened Zimmerman's self-defense claim. It is not unusual for witnesses when reinterviewed to remember new details, reconcile inconsistencies, and even contradict statements originally made. But the fact that all of these witnesses changed their original accounts that were made to the police when their memory of the event presumably was most fresh and they were not being interviewed by prosecutors who were trying to build a homicide case against Zimmerman raises the troubling implication that they were improperly coached. Here are the original accounts and altered versions of these witnesses (witness numbers used instead of real names):

WITNESS 1:

Original story: Witness saw two persons scuffle but didn't know "which one" was on top of the other during the scuffle.

New story: Witness says she is sure it was Zimmerman on top.

WITNESS 2:

Original story: Witness spotted Zimmerman with "blood on the back of his head." Zimmerman told this witness that Martin "was beating up on me, so I had to shoot him."

New story: Witness describes Zimmerman's demeanor as nonchalant, "More like, 'just tell my wife I shot somebody' like it was nothing."

WITNESS 3:

Original story: "I saw two guys running. Couldn't tell you who was in front, who was behind." After stepping away from her window, she said she looked again and "I saw a fistfight. Just fists. I don't know who was hitting who." In a second interview by police, she stated that during the chase, the two figures were ten feet apart.

> New story: She did not see two people running, just one person, whom she heard more than saw. "I couldn't tell you if it was a man, a woman, a kid, black, or white. I couldn't tell you because it was dark and because I didn't have my contacts on or glasses. I just know I saw a person out there."
>
> WITNESS 4:
>
> Original story: Witness states that on the night of the shooting Martin was on top, "just throwing down blows on the guy, MMA-style." Witness also recalled that Zimmerman was calling for help.
>
> New story: Witness tells prosecution he isn't sure who was calling for help.

The changed accounts are dramatic. Were these witnesses improperly coached by prosecutors or their investigators to change their original accounts? Human memory is a tricky phenomenon and a longstanding subject of scientific study. To be sure, a person's memory is not like a video camera. It is not unusual for witnesses when reinterviewed about an event to remember new details, recall certain facts differently, and even forget and omit critical facts. Interviewing is a complex process that requires skill, patience, and objectivity. The fact that key witnesses in the Trayvon Martin case altered their original accounts by itself is not a reason to suspect improper conduct by the interviewers. However, the fact that all of these key witnesses changed their stories in ways that consistently appeared to strengthen the prosecution's case against George Zimmerman is curious, even troubling.

Those who follow trials and other litigation procedures in the United States generally agree that witness coaching is one of the "dark"—some even call it "dirty"—secrets in the U.S. adversary system. As discussed earlier in the book, there is no question that lawyers, police, and investigators coach witnesses. They do it to improve their strategic positions. They do it overtly and covertly. They give witnesses cues and suggestions to alter recollections, to fill in gaps in memory, resolve ambiguities, eliminate contradictions, sharpen language, create emphasis, and alter demeanor.

Lawyers representing private clients coach witnesses because they are partisans who want to win. But prosecutors are lawyers who do not have clients. The entire community is the prosecutor's "client." Prosecutors are supposed to seek justice, not victories. So one would think that coaching is a practice that a prosecutor more than any other lawyer would have a duty to avoid. But many reported cases describe how prosecutors have coached witnesses to give false, misleading, and exaggerated testimony to enhance their chances of getting a conviction, even the conviction of an innocent person.

That several key witnesses in the Trayvon Martin case changed their stories is troubling. Whereas most prosecutors seek to build strong cases, Special State Prosecutor Angela Corey may not have been a disinterested prosecutor seeking justice. She cultivated an image as a zealous champion of victims. She even prayed with the Martin family over their loss. Many prosecutors promote the image of a victim's avenger. But having such an aggressive victim-oriented profile suggests that Corey and her staff may have reinterviewed these witnesses not with the neutral purpose to seek the facts fairly and impartially but with the self-interested purpose of bringing murder charges against Zimmerman.

Consider the Probable Cause Affidavit filed by Corey which charged Zimmerman with second-degree murder. It contains several significant gaps in the proof that the prosecution would need to fill in order to get a murder conviction. The affidavit alleges in several places that Zimmerman "followed" Martin, "confronted" Martin, and "shot" Martin. But it says nothing about what happened between "followed," "confronted," and "shot." The original statements of the four witnesses would have filled these gaps with circumstantial evidence inconsistent with second-degree murder—witness 1 said that she didn't know who was on top during the fight; witness 4 said that Zimmerman was calling for help; witness 3 said she saw two persons running and then saw a fist fight. But after being reinterviewed by prosecutors, witness 1 said Zimmerman was on top; witness 4 said he didn't know who was calling for help; witness 3 suggested that she didn't see a fight, and that she barely saw but mostly heard only one person, not two.

Further, to any civilian witness a prosecutor and her agents wield considerable power, prestige, and influence.

Witnesses typically respect the prosecutor as a law enforcement expert who can be trusted to use facts responsibly and correctly. In such a setting, a prosecutor has a unique ability to persuade, suggest, intimidate, and manipulate a witness into altering his or her story. The witnesses in this case almost certainly knew that the prosecutor had been specially appointed to investigate the Trayvon Martin killing, that the case had attracted national attention, that there was the suggestion of a cover-up by the Sanford police to protect Zimmerman, and that these witnesses were being reinterviewed to assist the prosecution to bring criminal charges against Zimmerman.

Coaching does not often happen overtly. It most often happens covertly, subtly, and sometimes even unwittingly. Since the interviews were secret, we do not know the extent to which these witnesses may have been influenced by the prosecutor's comments, suggestions, and innuendos. The new fact added by witness 2—describing Zimmerman's demeanor moments after the shooting as nonchalant—is a questionable opinion as a matter of evidence law, highly prejudicial to Zimmerman, and very likely suggested in a leading manner by the interviewer. But absent any record of how a prosecutor or investigator may have interacted with the witness prior to and during the interviewing sessions, it is unlikely that improper coaching could be demonstrated. And even if the actual interview is recorded, as some of these interviews apparently were, there is no record of what transpired before the interview session, and what suggestions the interviewer may have made.

Looking back, the changes by these witnesses are a concern in this controversial case. Given the complex nature of memory, the ambiguity and uncertainty of "facts," and the distorting effects of being questioned and requestioned about an event, it is plausible that the recollection of these witnesses—the original and altered versions—may have been a combination of an inaccurately remembered, inaccurately reconstructed, and inaccurately retrieved recollection of the event. It is indeed possible that the changed recollections may have been attributable to an imagined memory. The fact that these witnesses gave inconsistent accounts could impair their credibility in the eyes of a jury. But if their newer versions are accepted by the jury, then the prosecutor's chances of getting a conviction would be significantly improved. One is left with the nagging suspicion that these witnesses may have been consciously manipulated by the prosecution to produce just that result.

The Most Critical Issue in the Zimmerman Trial—Whose Voice Was Screaming for Help?

One of the most critical pieces of circumstantial evidence in the Zimmerman murder trial was a cry for help moments before the fatal shot was fired. The so-called "cry for help" was recorded at the time a witness who heard the struggle made a 911 call to the police. Identifying the voice of the person who made that outcry, although not conclusive, would certainly be compelling evidence that it was made by the victim of the physical encounter rather than by the aggressor. If the person crying out was Martin, the recording could be used by the prosecution to disprove Zimmerman's claim that he shot Martin in self-defense. If the cry was made by Zimmerman, it would be highly relevant to corroborate Zimmerman's claim that he was being attacked and beaten by Martin when he shot him. So, to prove it was Martin's voice, the prosecution would have had to rely on Martin's family and friends to give their opinions identifying the voice. The prosecution would also have to rely on forensic experts to give their opinions that it was Martin's voice. To prove it was his voice, Zimmerman would have had to rely on his family and friends, and experts as well. And faced with conflicting opinions, a jury would have had to decide which opinion they believed.

There is no reason why the trial judge would preclude family and friends of Martin and Zimmerman from giving their opinions as to the voice of the person screaming, as long as those persons are familiar with the person's voice. However, there are many reasons why forensic experts should be precluded from giving their opinions identifying the voice. The media reported that several forensic experts volunteered their opinions that the voice on the tape was not Zimmerman's, and that it was Martin doing the screaming. But were these opinions reliable? Is there a scientific basis to support their analysis? Has the methodology used by these experts been subjected to review by other experts in voice analysis? Indeed, has the subject of voice identification through scientific analysis been accepted broadly by the scientific community, and by the courts?

Consider, for example, how one of these so-called experts used a technique called "biometric voice analysis" to compare Zimmerman's voice. Zimmerman's voice was recorded when he was speaking calmly to police dispatchers shortly before the shooting. The expert compared that voice with the screaming voice on the 911 tape. This expert then found a 48 percent match between the voices, concluding "with reasonable scientific certainty that it's not Zimmerman." Is this opinion entitled to any weight? First, what is biometric voice analysis anyway? Is it similar or different from voice identification through voice spectrography, commonly called a *voiceprint*, which has been studied for years but which most courts have not admitted into evidence because it lacks scientific reliability and acceptability. Another so-called expert gave the media his "strong opinion" that the voice was Trayvon Martin's "without a doubt." What was the basis for this expert's opinion? According to this expert, "The tone of the voice is a giveaway." He then added, "That's a young man's voice." Is this the kind of responsible and professional opinion that an expert is expected to give?

Elsewhere this book discusses junk science in the courtroom. The concern here is obvious. What is the scientific basis for these conclusions? Are they based on legitimate and well-established scientific principles? Or is this just mumbo-jumbo? What is the scientific foundation for biometric voice analysis? Would any court realistically allow an expert to give his or her own subjective conclusion about the "tone" of someone's voice? Would any court ever permit an expert to opine that the speaker is a young man? Or allow an expert to give an opinion about the gender or race of a speaker simply by hearing the voice? These are not examples of reliable scientific study, investigation, and analysis. They represent examples of junk science.

Sadly, there are numerous instances in which prosecutors get convictions by presenting false, fraudulent, and erroneous opinions by persons holding themselves out as experts. According to the National Registry of Exonerations, false and erroneous scientific evidence, based on the testimony of experts with suspect credentials and opinions, has led to the wrongful convictions of numerous defendants.

Moreover, it has been demonstrated empirically that juries typically believe experts more than any other witness. The expert usually is viewed by a jury with an aura of special reliability and trustworthiness. However, the records of contemporary criminal trials are replete with instances of fake science finding its way into a courtroom through the testimony of bogus experts that contain false, exaggerated, and erroneous conclusions that lack any scientific validity. Several of these experts have become notorious, and their pretentious opinions have masked fraudulent and reckless quackery. These experts have testified to blatantly groundless and unscientific opinions: astronomical estimates of hair comparisons without any scientific basis; "unique" characteristics of feet without any scientific basis; weapons that "indeed and without doubt" caused certain wounds; an opinion that an accidental fire was intentionally set, and other instances of faked fingerprints, faked autopsies, faked ballistics evidence, and faked breathalyzer readings.

Opinions by "voice experts" raise similar concerns. For example, whereas fingerprint and DNA evidence have unique and distinguishable characteristics, there does not appear to be any scientific basis for claiming, as one of the above voice experts did, that each individual's voice is unique. And anyway, there are so many marked differences that may occur among various groups of talkers that giving an opinion as to the identity of a voice "to a reasonable degree of scientific certainty" is blatantly misleading. Even using hedging terms like "probable" or "inconclusive" would be problematic, but certainly a much more accurate opinion. Other factors contribute to inaccurate and misleading opinions. Hearing a speaker's voice in a calm state and an emotional state, as one of the voice experts did, makes any informed comparison even more hazardous. Finally, published studies of voice identification under experimental conditions show very high rates of error. Indeed, a report by the National Academy of Sciences on forensic voice identification concludes that the scientific basis for making reliable voice identifications is extremely weak.

The FBI, as a result of the report, decided not to use forensic voice analysis for courtroom evidence, although as with polygraph evidence, it continues to use it for investigative purposes.

The judge in the Zimmerman trial allowed the jury to hear the 911 call of a person's screams for help, and allowed a prosecution witness—a friend of Martin's—to testify that the voice was Martin's. But the judge refused to allow experts to testify to the identity of the voice, ruling that such testimony lacked a reliable scientific basis.

The Prosecution's Biggest Mistake in the Zimmerman Trial

As the Zimmerman trial came to an end, and observers and pundits started to predict the result, one significant question stood out starkly, unanswered, and elusive. Why did the prosecution decide to introduce in its own case the several audio and video statements made by George Zimmerman to the police after he shot and killed Trayvon Martin? Clearly, these recorded statements could not have been introduced into evidence by the defense. Out-of-court statements are hearsay, even if made by a defendant, and under one of the most well-established rules of evidence, are not admissible unless there is an exception. The only way Zimmerman's statements could have been introduced into evidence and considered by the jury is if the prosecution introduced the statements themselves, or somehow opened the door to allow the defense to use them. The best example of a prosecutor introducing a defendant's statements would be to offer a defendant's confession or other incriminating statements into evidence. Such proof is admissible under a familiar exception to the rule against hearsay, namely, the admissibility of a party's statements—called "admissions"—but only when they are offered by the opposing party.

To be sure, Zimmerman's defense team at an early stage of the proceedings released to the media Zimmerman's audio and video statements that described in Zimmerman's own words his encounter with Martin, and essentially formed the basis for Zimmerman's claim of self-defense. But the truthfulness of Zimmerman's account of the event, and Zimmerman's credibility, was never directly challenged at the trial. Since he did not testify, he could not be subjected to the foremost technique in our legal system to get at the truth—cross-examination. But even though the prosecution could have prevented the jury from hearing Zimmerman's narrative, it chose not to do so. The prosecution allowed Zimmerman's statements to be heard by the jury, and his demeanor seen by the jury when he made those statements, but without the prosecution being able to confront and cross-examine Zimmerman in court about these statements. The prosecution thereby made its biggest mistake in the trial.

Zimmerman's statements to the police lay the groundwork for the claim of self-defense. Without Zimmerman's statements the defense could only have proved his claim by statements from witnesses and the physical evidence at the scene. Zimmerman's statements corroborated his claim in a powerful way. His statements contained numerous self-serving references to previous break-ins in the gated community, the need to start a watch program in the neighborhood, Zimmerman's involvement as watch commander, how Zimmerman spotted Martin behaving suspiciously, how Martin fled to a darkened area and disappeared between houses, how Zimmerman dropped his phone, got punched in the face by Martin, had his head slammed into the concrete sidewalk, felt like his head was "going to explode," shouted for help several times, was told by Martin, "You're gonna die tonight, mother[expletive]," how Zimmerman became terrified, and prayed to God that someone might have videotaped his encounter with Martin. Zimmerman's demeanor on the video is calm, polite, forthcoming, and nonconfrontational. He looks like he's telling the truth. And the prosecution was not able to challenge his story.

Indisputably, without Zimmerman's recorded statements the prosecution's case was legally sufficient for a jury to convict, if not of murder, then arguably of manslaughter. The prosecution's case consisted of Zimmerman's apparent targeting and profiling of Martin, pursuing Martin while uttering expletives, continuing to pursue Martin after Zimmerman was directed by a police operator not to do so, and Martin, sounding fearful, telling his girlfriend over the phone that he was being pursued by a "creepy" man, then

Martin crying for help and shouting "Get off, get off," and during the ensuing struggle being shot and killed by Zimmerman. Witnesses observed portions of the struggle, and in differing and sometimes contradictory accounts provided circumstantial evidence to support and refute Zimmerman's claim of self-defense. But absent Zimmerman's statements to the police, it would have been far more difficult for the defense to prove that Zimmerman was justified in killing Martin, an unarmed young man who was returning home from the store when he was killed by Zimmerman.

It is hard to quantify what probative value was gained by the prosecution in introducing Zimmerman's statements. To be sure, the prosecution was able to point out several discrepancies in Zimmerman's accounts, but these were really minor inconsistencies. By introducing Zimmerman's statements, the prosecution paid a steep price. As noted above, it forfeited any opportunity to cross-examine Zimmerman because Zimmerman's description of what happened was now before the jury. He didn't have to testify to make out his claim of self-defense; his un-cross-examined statements to the police did that for him. Moreover, without Zimmerman's recorded statements that it was he who cried for help, it would have been much less likely that the voice on the 911 audio recording screaming for help would be attributed by the jury to Zimmerman. Moreover, his statements laid the groundwork for the testimony of the forensic pathologist that Martin's injuries were consistent with Zimmerman's account of the shooting.

It would have been interesting, assuming the prosecution chose not to introduce Zimmerman's statements, to speculate on whether the defense would have chosen to call Zimmerman to testify in his own defense. Assuming he testified, and gave testimony similar to his statements to the police, his credibility would then have been subjected to attack: Didn't he lie before to the court? What was it about Martin that made him "suspicious?" What other persons in the neighborhood did Zimmerman deem "suspicious?" What made him leave his car? He knew he was armed with a gun, didn't he? Did he think he might need to use it? What made him decide to follow Martin? Why didn't he heed the police directive not to pursue Martin? What made him feel so threatened? Did he really yell for help? At what point did he draw his gun? How serious were his injuries? Describe with a bit more detail how Martin kept bashing his head into the concrete? Did he lose consciousness? Go to a hospital?

On balance, the prosecution made a tactical blunder in allowing the jury to consider Zimmerman's account. The evidentiary benefits this gave to the defense were enormous, particularly in forfeiting any opportunity to confront Zimmerman directly, face-to-face, to attempt to discredit his story.

Late Saturday night, July 13, 2013, after deliberating for over sixteen hours, the jury found Zimmerman not guilty.

Chapter Five

The People of the State of New York v. Dominique Strauss-Kahn

The Strange Case of Dominique Strauss-Kahn

Dominique Strauss-Kahn was a prominent international celebrity and poised to be elected president of France when he was forcibly taken off his Paris-bound flight on May 14, 2011, and arrested by New York City police for raping a chambermaid in his hotel room earlier that day. The victim, Nafissatou Diallo, was a thirty-two-year-old immigrant from the West African state of Guinea. She claimed that Strauss-Kahn forced her to perform sexual acts on him, and DNA evidence from Diallo's clothes matched Strauss-Kahn. Bail was denied at the prosecution's request, but after he was indicted another judge set the bail at $1 million with onerous home detention and monitoring requirements.

As it turned out, Strauss-Kahn was probably innocent, or at least not guilty beyond a reasonable doubt. Diallo's story eventually was discredited, but so was Strauss-Kahn's reputation by the unrelenting media coverage. Indeed, the case became a worldwide sensation within a week. It appeared on the front page of more than 150,000 newspapers worldwide, and articles included the victim's name and lurid details of her private life. She brought a civil lawsuit against Strauss-Kahn which heightened the publicity.

However, three months after he was indicted, Strauss-Kahn's case was dismissed at the prosecution's request. The prosecution's decision was based on numerous inconsistencies in Diallo's story, the existence of physical evidence which contradicted Diallo's account of force and nonconsent, and her untruthfulness in claiming she was gang-raped in her native Guinea in order to gain asylum to the United States. Diallo's civil lawsuit against Strauss-Kahn was settled for $1.5 million.

Why Did the Prosecutors Request Such High Bail?

The media frenzy surrounding the arrest of Dominique Strauss-Kahn for sexually assaulting a chambermaid in his Manhattan hotel continued for several months and did not abate. A grand jury indicted him for several counts of sexual assault and his freedom was curtailed under extremely rigorous bail conditions. The serious felony charges would give even a guilty man pause for considering fleeing the jurisdiction.

When he was arrested in his first-class seat aboard a plane about to take off to Paris, the district attorney—feeding the media circus—demanded that Strauss-Kahn be remanded to jail instead of being allowed to post bail. The judge agreed, and Strauss-Kahn became an inmate at Riker's Island, New York City's version of France's notorious Devil's Island. The French press decried Strauss-Kahn's treatment by U.S. law enforcement, claiming, among other things, that denying him his liberty without any formal proof of guilt and the rush to judgment were monstrous injustices that disgraced the U.S. justice system in the eyes of the world.

The French made a good point. Why was Strauss-Kahn denied bail? Was the prosecution deliberating trying to intensify the media frenzy? As the prosecutors told the judge, Strauss-Kahn had been arrested on board an airline about to depart for France, a country that does not extradite its citizens. That reason alone may have influenced the prosecutors to claim that Strauss-Kahn presented a substantial risk of absconding before his trial, the most important reason for a judge to deny bail. However, the prosecutor's narrative of the relevant facts was at least misleading. The prosecutors knew that Strauss-Kahn had booked his flight about a week earlier, had called the hotel from the airport, and that after his arrest he offered to undergo extremely onerous bail conditions to ensure that he would not flee.

Indeed, reviewing his detention several days later, a different judge granted him bail, conditioned on Strauss-Kahn posting a $1 million bond, a $5 million insurance policy, surrendering his passport, wearing an electronic ankle bracelet to monitor his movements, restricting him to his apartment under supervision of a private investigation firm assigned by the court, and waiving extradition back to the United States if he managed to flee. So, a now fully informed judge made a seemingly reasoned and fair bail decision, a reminder to the world that the United States does indeed believe in due process, fair play, and justice, notwithstanding alleged conduct by an international celebrity that all people, including the French, would consider despicable if it turned out he was guilty.

However, the controversy surrounding Strauss-Kahn's bail raises a more fundamental question. What is it about the bail bond system in the United States that for many critics—including, judges, prosecutors, defense lawyers, and civic groups—is so odious, unfair, and indeed one of the dirty secrets in criminal law? Requiring a criminal defendant to post bail is legally permissible as long as it is reasonable. The U.S. Constitution in its Eighth Amendment states tersely: "Excessive bail shall not be required." But while bail typically is used to ensure that a person accused of a crime and who is released from custody returns to court to answer those charges, the courts have never held that there is a "right" to bail.

Nevertheless, the French critics make a valid point. Courts can refuse bail on a theory of preventive detention, by showing that the defendant is a "dangerous" person who likely will commit unlawful acts if he is released from confinement. Still, as a historical matter, bail has been about a defendant's risk of flight to avoid prosecution, and the reason high bail is imposed for someone like Strauss-Kahn is because he might pose a serious risk of fleeing given his abundant resources, not because there is any serious concern he would run amok in hotel rooms and sexually assault chambermaids.

However, the concept of a person charged with a crime and presumed innocent having to pay a fee to a bail bondsman to gain his or her freedom while awaiting trial is almost unheard of anywhere else in the world. In fact, in many countries, including England and Canada, an agreement to pay a defendant's bond for a fee is an obstruction of justice, similar to tampering with a witness or bribing a juror. Alternatives include deposits to the court, pledges of land or other property, and sworn promises to return to court.

The U.S. bail bond system has been shadowed by numerous well-documented accounts of serious abuses of bail by bondsmen. These weakly regulated businesses have been accused of retaining the collateral—cash or property—that persons must put up to get a bond, even though the bail bond people are required to return the collateral after the case is over. Bail bondsmen, some of whom fancy themselves as quasi-cops, can unilaterally decide if the defendant is a good bail risk, revoke the bond if they do not like the defendant's behavior, and thereby effectively put the defendant back in jail. If that happens, the bail bondsman gets to keep the fees. There's virtually no legal accountability, and the bail bond industry has proven difficult to regulate effectively.

Regulation of bail bond companies is made more difficult because what goes on between bail bondsmen and their clients occurs in private. In such a climate of secrecy, it is not surprising that allegations of corruption have clouded the commercial bail bond business, including accounts of collusion between bail bond companies, judges, prosecutors, and police officials. Then there are lurid stories of bond enforcement agents hired to capture persons who have failed to appear in court—so-called "bounty hunters"—who operate outside the legal system, and are notorious for breaking into people's homes without a warrant, holding innocent persons against their will, coercing statements, and forcibly taking people across state lines in violation of state extradition laws. The Constitution's Fourth Amendment does not apply to such bounty hunters because they are private citizens, not government officials.

Even more egregiously, there is the serious inequality that historically has haunted the bail system. As with so many other aspects of the criminal justice system, the kind of justice a person gets often depends on the amount of money he has. Indeed, every poor person charged with a crime gets a lawyer for free and has some modest opportunity to obtain investigative assistance and hire experts but not every defendant is a wealthy aristocrat like Strauss-Kahn who can afford to post a million dollar bond.

Most criminal defendants, in fact, are poor people who cannot afford bail and have insufficient resources to induce a bail bondsman to put up a bond. These defendants—accused of crimes but presumed innocent—remain incarcerated while awaiting trial, often for many months, and sometimes even for years. The prejudice to their cases from their inability to gain their liberty pretrial is extreme. Sitting in their jail cells, they have no ability to investigate their cases or assist their lawyers except in a limited and superficial way. When the defendant enters the courtroom from his cell, he stands before the jury not as a free citizen walking into court from the community but attired in prison garb and surrounded by correction officials to ensure he does not flee.

Worst of all, far too many of these poor defendants may in fact be innocent but calculate that it may be in their best interest to plead guilty. Why? Because given the high and unaffordable bail, they are forced to languish in jail for extended periods of time awaiting trial. They recognize the logic that even if they are acquitted after trial, they would have served considerable jail time for nothing. Thus, some defendants at their arraignment who cannot afford bail are advised by the prosecutor: "plead guilty now and I will recommend a sentence of thirty days; if not, we'll adjourn the case for forty-five days for your lawyer to make pretrial motions." The fact that an innocent defendant faced with such a harsh choice often pleads guilty is not surprising but is nonetheless unconscionable.

The ultimate bail result that Strauss-Kahn received was the correct one—even if the evidence against him was weak.

Given the severe restrictions placed on him, it is unlikely he would flee. Still, the controversy surrounding Strauss-Kahn should cause criminal justice experts, especially prosecutors, to rethink how our bail system works for the average defendant in the United States. And frankly, these experts do not need any help from the French.

Are Crime Victims Always Credible?

Nafissatou Diallo alleged that Dominique Strauss-Kahn rushed at her, grabbed her, tried to rape her, and forcibly compelled her to have sex with him, and that shortly thereafter, she made a criminal complaint against him. However, as the prosecutors and investigators continued to probe her story, they began to question the accuracy of her story. She made several contradictory statements as to what she did immediately after the event. But there is no dispute that her complaint was prompt, her accusation graphic and emotional, and there was physical evidence to corroborate her account.

Diallo had a conversation the next day with a friend who was an inmate in an immigration detention facility. The conversation was overheard by officials there. During this conversation, there was a reference to the fact that Strauss-Kahn was a wealthy man and that Diallo could profit financially from the sexual encounter. Although there are conflicting accounts of exactly what was said, and who raised the subject of Strauss-Kahn's ability to pay Diallo big bucks, it is possible that Diallo was the one who first raised the subject. Here is the question: Unless a victim of a vicious crime is independently wealthy, or wants only vengeance and significant punishment for her abuser, what law-abiding crime victim would not want to be compensated for such a brutal and humiliating attack?

Nevertheless, based on Diallo's apparent interest in seeking money from Strauss-Kahn, the tabloids and probably much of their readership concluded that Diallo was fabricating her claim of sexual abuse. Although there were other problems with Diallo's credibility - lying in her U.S. asylum application by claiming she was gang-raped in her former country, having a suspicious financial relationship with the inmate, and details in her story about what she did before she made her complaint against Strauss-Kahn changed—it is her alleged quest for money that most disturbed the media and the public and prejudiced them against her. She was pilloried in effect for allegedly wanting Strauss-Kahn to pay her for what he did to her.

Most defendants who commit violent crimes cannot afford a lawyer, bail, or investigators, and certainly do not have the ability to compensate their victims. That is one of the significant differences between the Diallo-Strauss-Kahn case and most other cases involving violent crimes, particularly sex crimes. Strauss-Kahn was a wealthy man. He plainly was able to compensate his victim in the same way that celebrities Michael Jackson and Kobe Bryant did. They paid handsomely to the persons who claimed to have been sexually abused by them. It is also probably correct that a typical crime victim does not have a financial motive the day after the offense. Victims typically are in a state of shock and physical distress but when the trauma subsides, victims may come to realize (perhaps with the assistance of a lawyer) that they should indeed seek a financial recovery from the offender who brutally violated them and who is in a position to compensate them.

There is no question that prosecutors understandably are concerned about a crime victim who seeks money from the perpetrator. Indeed, there is an unwritten policy among prosecutors that victims and witnesses must never mention wanting money out of a case. Prosecutors caution crime victims and their attorneys to wait until the criminal case is over before filing a civil lawsuit against the defendant. Prosecutors even admonish victims to not even talk about the possibility of a potential civil lawsuit.

Are prosecutors suppressing the truth? Clearly, prosecutors want to create an imaginary narrative for juries that the crime victim seeks only justice against the wrongdoer and does not have any pecuniary incentive in mind. Surely the prosecutor does not ask the victim to lie or mislead. The prosecutor simply asks the victim not to present to the defense lawyer on a silver platter the kind of ammunition that Strauss-Kahn's lawyers were afforded in the event the case went to trial, namely, that even if Diallo did not have a financial motive on the day of the alleged attack, she surely had one when at his trial she got on the witness stand

and testified. In fact, the subject of Diallo's wanting money from Strauss-Kahn consumed much of the discussion when Diallo's attorney met with members of the Strauss-Kahn defense team prior to trial to discuss a settlement.

A criminal trial ideally is intended to discover the truth about a past event where the facts are unclear, ambiguous, and hotly contested. Defense lawyers are allowed, even required, to attack the crime victim with sharp and aggressive questions, especially questions about a victim's possible motive to lie. Most crime victims may have no motive to lie but some do. Successful impeachment of a witness often has nothing to do with the merits of a case; rather, it is often about a witness's overall character and credibility. If a witness lies or misleads about some things, even peripheral matters, it is logical for the jury to infer that the witness may also be lying about the central and contested facts of the case. Cross-examination has been aptly described as the most powerful technique ever invented for exposing the truth.

So, if Diallo lied to the prosecutors in denying that she planned to seek money from Strauss-Kahn, that misrepresentation, along with other discrediting facts, might cause the prosecutors to conclude that she may have fabricated her account of the sexual attack. On the other hand, if the prosecutors are troubled because they are stuck with a crime victim who may have acknowledged, in an unguarded moment, that she saw the possibility of getting rich when the criminal case was over, it is probably high time for prosecutors to accept the fact that financial recoveries in criminal cases are sometimes a reality, and should not try to hide or obscure that fact through secrecy or disingenuousness.

Of course, defense lawyers are free to refer to a victim's financial motive in challenging the truthfulness of the witness's testimony but jurors should also be free to use their own experience and common sense when assessing the victim's credibility. The prosecutor should forcefully argue that crime victims have a right to be compensated for their pain and suffering, and such compensation should be no reason for the jury to disbelieve them. The prosecutor should explain to the jury that there is nothing inconsistent between a crime victim seeking justice in a criminal courtroom and also seeking justice in a civil tort proceeding. The jury should be instructed that crime victims have a legal right to compensation for their pain, abuse, and embarrassment, and that because they intend to pursue their right to be compensated to the fullest extent of the law, that should not be a reason to disbelieve them.

Only two people knew what happened in Strauss-Kahn's hotel room. If the prosecutors did not believe Diallo, they should not prosecute the case. However, if the prosecutors were convinced that she was forcibly attacked and compelled to perform a sexual act upon Strauss-Kahn, then they should not abandon the case even though a jury might not overlook her credibility problems.

It is ethically proper for prosecutors to proceed to trial even with a weak case that they believe stands a decent chance of losing if they believe in good faith that the defendant is guilty and that they have sufficient evidence to prove his guilt. That is exactly what a prosecutor's duty to serve justice really means. More than any other government official, a prosecutor is sworn to do just that.

Prosecutors Playing God

It would have been a classic courtroom battle—Nafissatou Diallo, a poor immigrant chambermaid, against Dominique Strauss-Kahn, a wealthy and powerful international celebrity, whom she accused of sexually attacking her. She told her dramatic story to virtually everyone: on TV, at press conferences, in interviews. However, there is one small group of people to whom she did not recount her story but who mattered most—a jury. Should there have been a trial by jury? Should the New York district attorney take the case to trial and ask the jury to render a verdict? Or should the prosecutor decide all by himself not to bring the case to trial? These questions go to the heart of the prosecutor's power and discretion.

Apart from the potentially dramatic David/Goliath confrontation, the case illustrates a fundamental ethical dilemma for a prosecutor. If a prosecutor believes that the victim is telling the truth, but also believes that there are strong reasons why a jury might reject her testimony, should the prosecutor allow the jury to hear the victim's story? Or, if the prosecutor believes a jury might acquit the defendant, should the prosecutor dismiss the case himself? Surely there is no legal or ethical problem if the prosecutor does not believe the victim, even though the prosecutor believes that a jury might convict. That was the issue confronting North Carolina prosecutor Michael Nifong in the Duke Lacrosse case, in which three Duke student-athletes were accused of raping a young woman at a fraternity party. Nifong decided to push on with the prosecution even though it was obvious to almost everybody, including himself, that the alleged victim was lying. Should a prosecutor take away a case from a jury when the evidence is weak, even though the prosecutor believes the defendant is guilty?

The evidence that Strauss-Kahn committed a criminal act, which originally appeared so ambiguous and conflicting when reported in the media-saturated blogs and tabloids, would have been far more focused and possibly incriminating if the proof was presented inside a courtroom. Consider, for example, the medical and scientific evidence to prove the attack. One of the arguments by Strauss-Kahn's lawyers was that the evidence of a forcible encounter was inconclusive and proved only that there was some type of sexual encounter, but not an aggressive and nonconsensual one. This claim, however, was advanced based on sketchy medical reports alone. The medical and scientific witnesses who wrote these reports were yet to testify. Their testimony would lend powerful support to Diallo's detailed description of the encounter. These expert witnesses likely would be able to identify specific bruises and abrasions on Diallo's body, particularly in the vaginal area, and would likely testify that in their opinion these injuries were consistent with a violent sexual attack and inconsistent with a consensual encounter.

Strauss-Kahn's lawyers would have a hard time refuting these opinions, particularly when the physical evidence appeared to interlock with the victim's account. Moreover, the defense was forced to concede from the outset that there was a sexual encounter. This concession was based on the discovery of Strauss-Kahn's semen on Diallo's body and clothing, and the defense of consent might ring hollow with a jury. As the prosecutor would likely argue in summation, "Why in the world would this woman consent to this man's offensive overtures?"

The prosecutor would also be able to introduce evidence from witnesses to whom Diallo cried for help shortly after the encounter. This evidence is labeled "Prompt Outcry" proof and is routinely admitted to corroborate that a forcible and unconsented sexual act in fact occurred. The theory is that if a victim complains immediately after a sexual attack, it is likely that the victim is telling the truth. If the act was consensual, why would a victim make an immediate complaint? More than the promptness of her complaint, however, would be the likely testimony from these witnesses as to Diallo's demeanor as she recounted the event. If she appeared shaken, crying, anguished, and clearly not in control of her emotions, the prosecutor would likely ask the jury: "Was this an act? Is this a game? Why would she make this up?"

Also, there appears to have been several previous similar instances in which Strauss-Kahn took sexual advantage of younger women, quite similar to the Diallo encounter. If this evidence was accessible to the prosecution, then introducing it would have a powerful impact on the jury. Such proof would strongly negate the defense of consent and likely reinforce the jury's conclusion that Diallo was telling the truth. Proof of prior similar sexual attacks unquestionably is highly prejudicial, and trial judges monitor such evidence carefully to ensure that it is offered for a legitimate purpose that outweighs its obvious prejudice. The purpose of such proof in the Diallo case would be to negate the defendant's claim of consent and show that Strauss-Kahn intended to have his way with Diallo that followed his long-standing pattern of his aggressive sexual behavior with younger women.

Then there would be the testimony of Diallo herself. Obviously she herself could make the case for guilt if she was able to convince twelve jurors beyond a reasonable doubt. This eventuality, obviously, is the biggest obstacle to prosecution and depends entirely on the judgment of the district attorney. The defense would attempt to discredit her testimony by showing that she made many contradictory statements, that she fabricated a claim of rape to gain entry into the United States, and that she demanded money from Strauss-Kahn.

However, judging by her public appearances and statements, she was a poised, articulate, and passionate young woman who, when sitting confidently on the witness stand—finally getting her "day in court," so to speak—would be capable of convincing a jury that what she claimed to have happened to her really did happen. Her demeanor on the witness stand would be a key element in the jury's decision on whether she is to be believed. Her report to the police investigators after the encounter was so detailed, emotional, and convincing that it made the decision to arrest immediately such a distinguished and powerful international celebrity a reasonable one.

Proving guilt in the U.S. criminal justice system places a huge burden on a prosecutor. Some prosecutors violate rules in order to get a jury to find guilt, as prosecutor Nifong tried to do. Some prosecutors take an easier route by offering the defendant a favorable plea bargain. Some prosecutors decide to drop cases entirely. Since no plea deal was acceptable to Strauss-Kahn, the question of whether the district attorney would drop the case or go to trial needed to be resolved. Should the prosecutor play God and decide on his own that given the weakness of the proof that no jury likely would convict? Should the prosecutor play God and decide that it would be unjust to force Strauss-Kahn to trial in light of the contradictory evidence and the possibility that he might be innocent? Or should the prosecutor allow this controversial case that captivated the attention of the public both locally and around the world to be presented to an impartial jury, in a public courtroom, in a fair and objective manner, with all the procedural protections our system offers, and without the intervention of the media to influence the jury's decision, and then, as trial lawyers say, let the chips fall where they may? That sounds like a prosecutor promoting justice.

The Aftermath

The case ended in an unusual way. Dominique Strauss-Kahn returned to France a free man and was acclaimed by some people for his triumph over the shameful behavior of the U.S. criminal justice system. Whether in fact he is guilty of a violent attack on a hotel chambermaid no longer mattered. The "alleged" victim (one must continue to use the word "alleged") was exposed by the prosecutors as a serial liar on numerous matters. Whether she also lied about the ultimate issue in the case, namely, whether she was forced to have sex with Strauss-Kahn, is now beside the point. She did irreparable damage to her own credibility and, perhaps more importantly, to rape victims everywhere. They will now know the cost of coming forward with rape complaints when it is they, perhaps even more than the defendant, who will become the accused.

It does not matter whether it was the prosecutors, the media, or the defense attorneys who discovered Nafissatou Diallo's litany of lies. It appears that the prosecutors themselves either became suspicious or were told of some problems in her story by her own attorney. It was inevitable that Strauss-Kahn's attorneys would be armed at trial with powerful and damning exculpatory evidence: the false claims Diallo made in her asylum petition; her phony tax deductions; her false account of hiding out just before she complained; her relationship with a drug dealer; her multiple telephone numbers; her suspicious deposits to her bank account; and her recorded bragging that she knew how to deal with the "rich guy."

The case was a media bonanza. The French press even printed the victim's name, something that would never occur but for Strauss-Kahn's status. The prosecutors knew that identifying her would yield extremely damaging personal information about her. And in this "rich man's case," the defense had unlimited resources to investigate her credibility with or without the assistance of the media. And the prosecutors surely knew how deadly that combination can be for a successful prosecution.

As the dust settled over this case, one can reflect on some lessons for prosecutors, and future prosecutors. Consider the way prosecutors can be so quick and so determined to accuse, indict, and convict a person in the court of public opinion. The prosecutors ordered a quick arrest, demanded that the defendant's liberty be taken away and that he be held in jail without bail awaiting trial, and then gave inflammatory information to the media insinuating the defendant's guilt. It is also important to reflect on the gross disparity of resources in American justice between the rich and poor. The anonymous person on the street who is arrested and accused of a serious crime and later exonerated does not typically see prosecutors coming forward with remorse and apologies for rushing to bring an accusation before they know all the facts. Particularly if the person on the street was quickly indicted, as Strauss-Kahn was, his case would probably languish for many months, even years, with him behind bars waiting for justice.

Moreover, the New York district attorney knew what he would be up against in court. He knew the high quality of the attorneys who would ultimately be interrogating Diallo in court and knew that the international media would be watching. It is irrelevant whether the source of the victim's lies originated with the media, defense counsel, or from the prosecutors themselves. Prosecutors typically do not relish prosecuting even a guilty defendant if they know they are almost surely going to lose.

The real question is the impact this case may have had on the rest of the criminal justice docket. That the district attorney came forward to acknowledge his rush to judgment is surely a good thing, even if it cannot repair the injustice to the accused. Rushes to judgment are never a good thing, even if done for a legitimate reason—in this case, the legal requirement to obtain a quick indictment of Strauss-Kahn to ensure that he would not abscond.

What about the other not so prominent defendants with long rap sheets represented by barely competent attorneys who are overburdened with portfolios of hundreds of other cases? Most defendants charged with violent crimes cannot afford bail, certainly not the million dollars that Strauss-Kahn posted. These defendants would remain in jail for months or years, even if innocent. With such large case-loads themselves, how many prosecutors would have had the time and resources to so carefully scrutinize the victim's background and credibility to determine if she is telling the truth? This kind of in-depth investigation typically happens on the eve of a trial, not weeks after an arrest. Most likely, the prosecutors would simply have done what is commonly done when problems with a victim's credibility appear: offer the accused a cheap plea and get the case off the docket.

L'Affaire Strauss-Kahn is a criminal justice scandal, but a scandal that could provide important insights in the way cases are prosecuted, and the consequences when prosecutor make bad judgments.

While Nafissatou Diallo quietly owns and operates a West African restaurant in New York City, Dominique Strauss-Kahn battled other charges in France. He was acquitted in 2015 of pimping charges relating to his participation in orgies in Paris, Brussels, and Washington, DC, with prostitutes from 2008 to 2011.

Chapter Six

Hiding Evidence

Brady Stories

Brady v. Maryland is the landmark Supreme Court decision holding that constitutional due process requires prosecutors to disclose to defendants favorable evidence that is material to guilt or punishment. The "Brady Rule" was intended to make trials less like a sporting contest and more about ensuring that justice is done under fair and civilized rules. However, after more than fifty years, Brady violations have become one of the most pervasive forms of prosecutorial misconduct, described by one court as having reached "epidemic" levels.

The stories below describe notable cases in which prosecutors hid critical evidence from defendants, which could have proven their innocence. These stories reveal the mindset of prosecutors faced with a legal and ethical challenge under Brady. Assume the prosecutor is confident the defendant is guilty, has sufficient evidence to prove the defendant's guilt, and, as with any advocate, wants badly to win a conviction. To this prosecutor, the Brady duty is counter-intuitive; why disclose to a defendant evidence that might be used to defeat the prosecutor in his or her pursuit of justice?

Of course this mindset begs the question: Should a prosecutor's confidence in the defendant's guilt excuse the prosecutor from his disclosure obligation? The defendant is presumed innocent and guilt must be proven to a jury's satisfaction, not the prosecutor's. Moreover, the prosecutor's paramount duty is not merely to win a conviction but to prosecute fairly and responsibly. Not surprisingly, many convictions of innocent persons have been the result of the prosecutor's failure to disclose exculpatory evidence that would have proven the defendant's innocence.

The cases in this chapter offer insights into how prosecutors view their Brady obligations. To test the hypothesis that prosecutors either don't understand what Brady requires, or refuse to honor the rule, my law school's clinic on domestic violence surveyed New York State prosecutors supervising domestic violence prosecutions in which the defendant was charged with assault, aggravated harassment, and menacing. Prosecutors were asked whether they would disclose to the defense statements made by a hypothetical victim. Sixty-two questionnaires were sent out and thirty-two prosecutors' offices responded. Prosecutors were asked whether the following statements by the victim were Brady evidence that needed to be disclosed:

1. "It was all my fault." Twelve prosecutors said it was Brady; twelve said it was not Brady.
2. "I instigated the whole encounter." Ten said it was Brady; thirteen said it was not Brady.
3. "I made him hit me." Twelve said it was Brady; twelve said it was not Brady.
4. "He didn't hurt me." Twenty-three said it was Brady; seven said it was not Brady.
5. "I hit him too." Fourteen said it was Brady; fourteen said it was not Brady.
6. "I exaggerated what happened." Eighteen said it was Brady; ten said it was not Brady.
7. "What's in the police report isn't true." Twenty-three said it was Brady; three said it was not Brady

I was surprised by the responses. I assumed that every prosecutor surveyed would have disclosed every statement. I assumed as well that any court reviewing these statements would conclude that Brady required prosecutors to disclose these statements.

The cases discussed below are far from hypothetical. They are tragic examples of prosecutors hiding powerful evidence of innocence which, had it been disclosed to the defendant, likely would have changed the result. Instead, the decision by the prosecutors to hide the evidence destroyed the right of these defendants to receive a fair trial, and doomed them and their families to years of needless suffering.

The Case of Michael Morton

Former Texas prosecutor, and later Judge Ken Anderson, was recently disbarred and jailed after he was found by a disciplinary tribunal to have deliberately suppressed exculpatory evidence that sent an innocent man to prison for twenty-five years. Anderson, the prosecutor in the 1987 murder trial of Michael Morton, protested that "the system screwed up" and that he did nothing wrong. He appeared more anguished over protecting his own image and "what me and my family have been through for eighteen months of false accusations" than the tragedy he caused by abusing his power as a prosecutor and destroying most of the life of an innocent man. Arrogant, defiant, and dishonest, Anderson's misconduct in Morton's trial, and his attempt to justify his deceit of court, jury, and defense counsel, typifies the worst in prosecutors.

Michael Morton was accused of murdering his wife, Christine, by bludgeoning her to death with a wooden bar in their Williamson County home in 1986 before going to work. The killing attracted considerable attention—"It was a big deal" according to former prosecutor Kimberly Gardner who worked under Anderson. The evidence of Morton's guilt was circumstantial and weak. Anderson's theory was that Morton killed his wife because she wouldn't have sex with him, and the medical examiner provided an opinion that tried to pinpoint, but with questionable accuracy, the time of death as occurring before Morton left for work.

However, there was considerable evidence that strongly supported the defense theory that a stranger entered the Morton home and killed Christine after Michael left. Almost all of this exculpatory evidence was contained in notes, reports, and transcripts gathered by the lead investigator, Sgt. Don Wood, of the Williamson County Sheriff's Office.

The information collected by Wood, which he shared with Anderson, included the following: reports from neighbors seeing a man in a green van behind the Morton home at the time of Christine's murder; the transcript of an interview by Sgt. Wood of Rita Kirkpatrick, Morton's mother-in-law, stating that her three-year-old grandson Eric told her he saw a "a monster," not his father, beat his mother to death; evidence that Christine's purse was stolen, as well as her credit card and checkbook being fraudulently used several days later; unidentified fingerprints in the Morton home; and an unidentified footprint in the backyard. It is difficult not to believe that if Morton's lawyers had this evidence, they would have been able to persuade the jury that substantial reasonable doubt existed of Morton's guilt. But the jury never learned about this evidence because Anderson hid it from Morton's lawyers and from the trial judge who had specifically ordered Anderson to disclose all evidence in his possession that was favorable to Morton.

One witness Anderson chose not to call was Sgt. Wood, the chief investigating officer who would have given the jury the background of the case and all of the evidence he accumulated, including the above evidence that contradicted

Morton's guilt. However, as Anderson knew, if he called Wood he would have been required to divulge all of Wood's case notes, reports, and the transcript of the child's statement describing the killer as a "monster." So, according to the testimony of a former prosecutor, Anderson stated he wasn't calling Wood because that way "the other side can't have access to those reports."

Equally egregious was Anderson's response to the 1987 order by the trial judge William Lott, since deceased, to disclose all of the evidence the police had collected. Anderson turned over a slender envelope containing only Morton's statements to the police; he did not disclose the mountain of evidence collected by Wood that would have strongly supported Morton's claim of innocence. It is this alleged violation by Anderson of the trial court's disclosure order that was one of the central issues at Anderson's disciplinary hearing.

In order to win a conviction, Anderson knew that he could not reveal to the defense the child's statements to his grandmother or the child's description of the killer. He knew this evidence would likely have doomed his prosecution. According to the testimony of a former prosecutor in his office, Anderson acknowledged to him: "The kid thinks a monster killed his mother," that his father was not present when his mother was killed, and the child's description of other details that corresponded to the evidence at the crime scene, including a blue suitcase that the killer placed atop his mother's body. Anderson stated that if the child's story ever got exposed, Anderson would claim that what the child really saw was his father dressed in a scuba diving suit as a disguise and that's why there was no blood on his clothing.

The former prosecutor recalled that Anderson's concoction of a story of "this guy killing his wife in front of his three-year-old son in a skin diving suit was pretty strange." What was Anderson's reason for not disclosing the child's statements to the defense? According to Anderson, "He was a traumatized three-year-old child. You can't attach any significance to anything he said." In other words, according to Anderson's view of acceptable prosecutorial practice, if a prosecutor learns that evidence exists that contradicts the prosecution's theory of guilt, that evidence, by definition, is mistaken, erroneous, or false. With such a mindset—similar to the fox guarding the henhouse—a prosecutor will always withhold evidence that might damage the prosecutor's case.

Interestingly, Anderson repeatedly professed in a deposition to not having any memory of the factual details of the Morton case, including the child's statement, or Anderson's bizarre scuba diving story to explain it. Is Anderson's failure to recall critical facts in the Morton case truthful or disingenuous? Anderson, in his book *Crime in Texas*, about which he was questioned at the disciplinary hearing, recounts how as a prosecutor, he had to master hundreds of details in cases, especially high-profile cases like Morton's.

Anderson pleaded no contest to the felony charges of criminal contempt of court. He was sentenced to ten days in jail and was stripped of his law license. The consensus in the community was that Anderson got off easy. The new district attorney promised to carefully review every case that Anderson ever prosecuted.

Michael Morton will have a special place in Texas criminal law. The Texas code of criminal procedure was recently amended to include a new Brady provision: "Prosecutors shall not suppress evidence or secrete witnesses capable of establishing the innocence of the accused." The new provision is called the "Michael Morton Act."

Morton today lives quietly with his wife in a small house in East Texas tucked away in pine trees beside a still lake. His son Eric, who was three when he watched his mother being murdered, visits him often. Eric lost his father too, for twenty-five years, because a prosecutor wanted to win a conviction too badly.

The "Grid Kid" Slaying

It was a sensational New York murder trial—the Grid Kid Slaying—in which two young men, John Giuca and Antonio Russo, reputed members of a Brooklyn street gang, were convicted in 2005 of killing a young college football player, Mark Fisher, after a night of drinking and partying in the city. Russo was the actual killer, and the evidence against him was strong. The case against Giuca, by contrast, was weak. Two friends testified that he told them he put Russo up to it, and gave Russo the gun, but their stories contradicted each other's, and their credibility was suspect. One of these witnesses has since recanted, claiming that the Brooklyn District Attorney's Office threatened to destroy her career unless she testified against Giuca.

However, it was a third witness, John Avitto, who was the prosecution's star. Avitto, a drug addict with a long criminal record, who faced seven years imprisonment for a burglary and had recently absconded from a drug treatment program, was called by the prosecutor on the last day of the trial, without any notice to the defense. Avitto, who was a jail-mate of Giuca's, testified that Giuca told him he had helped kill Fisher. Avitto told the jury that he did not receive anything for his testimony and that he just wanted to testify in order to do the right thing for the first time in his life. Avitto has since recanted his testimony and has apologized to Giuca but the damage, of course, was done.

Giuca has protested his innocence from the start, and has aggressively battled to overturn his conviction. His mother, in a highly publicized gambit, went undercover to try to expose misconduct by the jury. Giuca's principal litigation attack, however, was to show he did not receive a fair trial because of misconduct by the prosecutor.

Giuca's prosecutor was the chief of homicide trials, Anna Nicolazzi, who claimed she never lost a murder case. She accompanied Avitto into drug court after he was detained on a warrant, and after she conferred with the judge, Avitto was set free. Nicolazzi never disclosed to the defense that she had interceded on Avitto's behalf, or disclosed damaging information in Avitto's drug treatment and psychiatric records that would have raised substantial questions about Avitto's mental and emotional conditions. The prosecutor had a constitutional and ethical duty under *Brady v. Maryland* to disclose this information to the defense, but she claimed she did not know the details in these records and did not discuss Avitto's psychiatric and drug condition with the medical and drug officials who examined and treated him. She claimed she did not do so because she had no obligation to do so.

Is the prosecutor's claim that she did not ask the medical staff about Avitto's medical or drug history and current treatment credible? Is it reasonable to believe that a responsible prosecutor about to put her star witness on the stand would not have made even a superficial inquiry about Avitto's emotional and mental health? The records contained the following, which Nicolazzi claimed she knew nothing about: Avitto was suicidal and tried to commit suicide three times, once recently; he suffered from serious and persistent mental illnesses; he had fantasies and auditory hallucinations; he saw snakes; he heard voices, including voices ordering him to kill himself; he was bipolar; he suffered from posttraumatic stress disorder; he felt paranoid and took medication for mood disorders and anxiety; his memory was poor; he had a high level of distractibility; he admitted he lied to get preferential treatment in jail; he stated to the mental health officials that "I do what I have to do to change my situation."

At a recent hearing on Giucca's bid for a new trial, Nicolazzi told the court that she knew nothing about Avitto's mental and emotional impairments but acknowledged that such information would have helped Giuca's defense. She admitted that when she called Avitto to testify at the end of the trial she knew that Giuca's lawyer would not have been able to discover this information independently. Indeed, when Avitto took the stand and the defense requested any and all records of Avitto's psychiatric treatment and drug abuse, the prosecutor claimed she had no records, did not know about any records, and that there was no reason for her to search for records of Avitto's mental and drug history. The prosecutor even asserted that by seeking out this information she would have been violating Avitto's right to privacy, but she never asked Avitto to waive his right to privacy even though a defendant's fate hung in the balance. Why? Because, Nicolazzi maintained, she had no obligation to do so.

Consider this picture of a tough Brooklyn homicide prosecutor who claims that the right to privacy of a mentally and emotionally disturbed felon, a fugitive who had absconded from a drug program and had committed over a half-dozen other drug violations, outweighed the right of a young man charged with murder to a fair trial, and outweighed the prosecutor's duty to disclose to the defense any information that would have helped the defense attack the credibility of her star witness. Nicolazzi even asked Avitto at trial how he was doing in the drug program, and Avitto answered, "I'm doing good."

There are prosecutors, and there are good prosecutors. The goal of any prosecutor is to win; the goal of any good prosecutor is to do justice. Prosecutors ask a jury to convict if the evidence is legally sufficient; good prosecutors won't force a defendant to trial unless they are morally convinced of the truthfulness of their proof and of the defendant's guilt. Prosecutors won't look for evidence of innocence; good prosecutors will.

A prosecutor's claim of ignorance as an excuse for not complying with constitutional and ethical rules resembles a criminal defendant's claim of ignorance as an excuse to avoid criminal liability. For example, defendants charged with drug possession frequently claim they didn't know what was in the package they were carrying, or the car in which they were passengers. However, a trial judge, using the familiar "Ostrich" instruction, typically instructs a jury that a defendant may not avoid guilty knowledge by closing her eyes for fear of what she might learn, or burying her head in the sand so she will not be able to see or hear bad things. Why should a prosecutor be held to a less demanding standard? When a prosecutor has reason to believe that there is a strong probability that evidence exists that might free a defendant but deliberately looks the other way in order not to find it, the prosecutor should be deemed to know of its existence, and be held to have violated her duty of disclosure.

To compound her misconduct, the prosecutor, in her summation, vouched for Avitto's truthfulness. Here's what she told the jury: "Everything Avitto told you is credible"; "Avitto was being truthful"; "You can trust Avitto"; "Avitto was very honest"; "You know that Avitto isn't making it up." How, without knowing anything about Avitto's psychiatric and drug abuse history, could this prosecutor make these outlandish assertions about Avitto's truthfulness? The prosecutor became an Ostrich; she buried her head in the sand so she would not learn things that she would have to divulge to the defense and which might have impaired her chances of winning a murder conviction.

The big question is how many prosecutors play these perverse games?

Do Prosecutors Need Brady Training?

That's the message from the U.S. Supreme Court's strange decision in *Connick v. Thompson*, which vacated a $15 million dollar jury award for John Thompson, a Louisiana man who spent fourteen years on death row (in all, eighteen years in prison) for back-to-back armed robbery and murder convictions. Thompson was weeks away from being executed until an investigator found blood evidence on the robbery victim's clothing that proved Thompson's innocence (he was Type O, but the blood evidence was Type B). This evidence had been hidden from Thompson's lawyer by a team of prosecutors in the New Orleans District Attorney's Office. As one of these prosecutors told Thompson: "I'm going to fry you. You will die in the electric chair."

This grisly, almost unimaginable chapter in U.S. criminal justice history, has to rank as one of the court's most disturbing opinions on the Brady rule. Thompson, after his exoneration, brought a civil rights lawsuit against New Orleans district attorney Harry Connick. Thompson claimed that Connick was "deliberately indifferent" to the constitutional rights of defendants prosecuted by Connick's office. Indeed, one of Connick's prosecutors actually confessed to having deliberately suppressed the exculpatory blood evidence. There also was evidence that Connick knowingly allowed prosecutors in his office to engage in repeated acts of misconduct, especially withholding exculpatory evidence, without any adverse consequences. The Thompson case was the third in which the Supreme Court found Connick's office to have engaged in flagrant Brady violations.

Critical to Thompson's case, which the jury, as well as two lower federal courts, found persuasive, was proof that Connick willfully failed to train his prosecutors about how to handle Brady evidence. Connick's office, the civil jury learned, had one of the worst records in the country in handling such evidence. Astonishingly, Connick claimed that training his assistants on proper Brady practices would have made his job more difficult.

Agreeing that an office policy of deficient Brady training could establish a prosecutor's deliberate indifference, the Supreme Court majority nevertheless found that there was insufficient evidence of deficient training in Connick's office, but that even if there was such evidence, it would be irrelevant to whether Thompson's constitutional rights were violated.

The majority's reasoning was bizarre. The majority observed that whereas police officers need extensive training, for example, when they chase fleeing felons and need to know when they can use deadly force, prosecutors, by contrast, are lawyers who have been extensively trained in law school on how to interpret and apply legal rules and how to use evidence responsibly. Prosecutors have passed a bar examination demonstrating their fitness to practice law. Moreover, prosecutors receive abundant on-the-job training on how to use evidence. And anyway, according to the majority, the constitutional principle at stake in Thompson's case did not require special training; it was an aberrant act, the act of "one rogue prosecutor," and training would have made no difference.

The majority ignored, dismissed, or misstated the massive evidence presented to the civil rights jury that the absence of education and training in Connick's office contributed heavily to that office's culture of deliberate indifference to the rights of defendants, and that this dysfunctional office culture caused Thompson's horrific miscarriage of justice. This evidence was described in the powerful dissenting opinion of Justice Ruth Bader Ginsburg, who took the unusual step of reading her opinion from the bench. Her dissent was so contemptuous of the majority's decision that it provoked a gratuitous concurring opinion from Justice Scalia seeking to legitimize the majority opinion from Ginsburg's savage rebuke.

The Supreme Court knew that the misconduct under Connick's watch was neither isolated nor aberrant, nor the work of a few "rogue" prosecutors. There was massive evidence produced at Connick's civil rights trial that both Connick and the prosecutors in his office were ignorant of the constitutional rules regarding disclosure of Brady evidence. They also were ignorant of the rules regarding disclosure of scientific evidence. Connick's office had no training or continuing education, and no procedures to monitor compliance with Brady requirements. Prosecutors did not review police files. And shockingly, Connick himself had been indicted by federal prosecutors a few years earlier for suppressing a lab report of the type that was hidden from Thompson.

The culture of misconduct in Connick's office was not unfamiliar to the Supreme Court. A few years earlier, in *Kyles v. Whitley*, the court vacated a capital murder conviction also prosecuted by Connick's office based on the conduct of several unscrupulous prosecutors in hiding Brady evidence that, as in Thompson's case, sent an innocent man to the death chamber.

District Attorney Connick is now gone from the office. But what happened to John Thompson is not aberrant. It reflects the continuing vulnerability of defendants in the criminal justice system to miscarriages of justice when prosecutors lack education, skill, and training about fundamental rules of criminal procedure, or even more regrettably, are indifferent to it.

The Tragic Story of the "Hurricane"

Here comes the story of the Hurricane
The man the authorities came to blame
For something that he never done
Put him in a prison cell but one time he could have
been
The champion of the world.

"Hurricane," Bob Dylan

Rubin "Hurricane" Carter died in 2014. He emerged from the broken streets of Paterson, New Jersey, to become a symbol of the racial violence and urban upheaval inflaming the country in the 1960s. He was known as "Hurricane" for his ferocious power as a professional boxer. His life has been widely chronicled in literature, song, and film, largely because of the nineteen years he spent in a prison cell for murder, his heroic efforts at exoneration and freedom, and his scornful defiance of his jailers. Carter was found guilty of murdering three people in a Paterson, New Jersey bar in 1966. According to Dylan's anthem, Carter "was obviously framed, and couldn't help but make me feel ashamed to live in a land where justice is a game."

Whether Carter, along with John Artis, was guilty or innocent will never be known for certain. What is certain, however, is that as the courts found, Carter and Artis were denied fair trials because of the deliberate misconduct by the Passaic County prosecutors. Their convictions after the first trial were reversed by the New Jersey Supreme Court based on the prosecution's subornation of perjury from two key witnesses and concealment of crucial exculpatory evidence. Their convictions following their retrial were vacated by a federal district court based on the prosecutor's concealment, once again, of critical exculpatory evidence as well as his inflaming the jury with an appeal to racial prejudice.

The three victims—the bartender at the Lafayette Bar and Grill and two patrons—were gunned down by two black men at 2:30 a.m. on June 17, 1966. The victims were all white, and it was suspected to be retaliation for the shotgun murder earlier that night of a black tavern owner by a white man. Carter and Artis were stopped by police because the white sedan they were driving resembled the getaway car described by a witness. Carter and Artis were cleared; a patron in the bar who was wounded and another eyewitness told the police that Carter and Artis were not the killers. The two also had strong alibis and they both passed polygraph tests. They testified voluntarily in the grand jury.

A few months later, however, Carter and Artis were indicted for first-degree murder. They were identified by two new witnesses—Alfred Bello and Arthur Dexter Bradley—who were in the process of burglarizing a nearby building when they said they heard gunfire and saw Carter and Artis flee the tavern with guns. Without any proof of a motive, and despite their alibis, but based on Bello's and Bradley's testimony, the all-white jury convicted Carter and Artis.

Bello and Bradley lied. They lied about deals they made with the prosecution in exchange for their testimony, and they both recanted their testimony, claiming they were pressured by the prosecution to falsely accuse Carter and Artis. One powerful piece of evidence, which the prosecutor never disclosed to the defense, was a tape recording of an interview by the prosecutor's lead investigator—a member of the prosecutor's staff—with Bello. According to the transcript, Bello told the investigator he was unable to identify Artis and was not sure about Carter, or of the make of the car he had seen near the bar. However, as the interview progressed, and after the investigator makes numerous promises to Bello of lenient treatment for his pending crimes and his assistance in getting his parole dropped, Bello positively identified Artis and Carter. Three days later, he gave a written statement to the prosecution, again positively identifying Carter and Artis as the two men he saw fleeing from the bar. Bradley also was promised help with several pending charges and future sentencing. At trial, however, Bello and Bradley swore under oath that no promises were made to them while the prosecutor sat by silently, allowing these witnesses to commit perjury.

Carter's and Artis's retrial in 1976 featured only Bello as the prosecution's key witness; he had recanted his recantation prior to trial, but given Bello's dishonest testimony in the first trial, and his continued revisions of his story, his account according to one court "became unrecognizable." The prosecution thus faced a difficult challenge to win new convictions. The challenge appeared even more daunting because Bello swore in an affidavit in 1975 that he was "in the bar" when the shootings occurred, not outside the bar, as he had testified previously, and a polygraph expert retained by the prosecution concluded that Bello was telling the truth when he claimed he was "in the bar." Faced with this additional blow to Bello's credibility, the prosecutor concealed the polygraph expert's report and coached Bello to testify consistently with his testimony in the first trial. However, the prosecutor's suppression of the expert's conclusion was such a serious constitutional violation that Federal District Judge Lee Sarokin vacated the convictions, observing that "a more egregious violation is difficult to imagine." He ordered a new trial.

The prosecutor now needed to shore up his case some other way. There was no new proof. So, the prosecutor concocted a new theory to win convictions, the "racial revenge theory," as Judge Sarokin labeled it. This malevolent gambit sought to inflame the jury against Carter and Artis by claiming that the two killed the white bartender in retaliation for the killing of a black bar owner earlier that night. The prosecutor portrayed Paterson in the 1960s, like many other American cities, as inflamed with racial turmoil, race riots, and senseless violence. The prosecutor sought to exploit this history and the jury's racial fears and prejudices by imputing a motive for revenge on the entire black community, and thus onto Carter and Artis. Citing racial conflicts among Greeks and Turks and Irish (some of whom were on the jury), the prosecutor argued in his summation that "no group is immune from hate"; "revenge is one of the most powerful motives"; "what other reason could the murders have happened for?"

But there were significant problems with the prosecutor's approach. First, the race theory did not fully explain the killings of the two bar patrons who were black. More importantly, as Judge Sarokin noted, there was absolutely no proof against Carter and Artis to support the racial revenge theory. There was no evidence that either Carter or Artis knew that it was a white man who killed the black bar owner or that even if they knew, they would have reacted in such a vicious and violent manner. "In essence," Judge Sarokin observed, "the prosecution was permitted to argue to the jury that defendants who were black were motivated to murder total strangers solely because they were white."

In vacating Carter's and Artis's convictions and granting them their freedom, Judge Sarokin concluded: "For the state to contend that an accused has the motive to commit murder solely because of his membership in a racial group is an argument which should never be permitted to sway a jury or provide the basis of a conviction."

Dylan ends his hymn to Carter:

That's the story of the Hurricane
But it won't be over till they clear his name
And give him back the time he's done
Put him in a prison cell but one time he could a been
The champion of the world.

Ruben Carter spent nearly twenty years in prison. He was never officially exonerated for the murders. After his release he became an advocate for the wrongfully convicted. He wrote in an Op Ed piece two months before his death that his dying wish was for Brooklyn prosecutors to exonerate David McCollum of a murder Carter said McCollum did not commit. Carter died on April 20, 2014. McCollum was exonerated six months later.

Destroying a U.S. Senator

Senator Ted Stevens was convicted in 2008 for making false statements on senate financial disclosure forms. Shortly after his conviction, serious irregularities in the prosecution of his case prompted the Department of Justice to assign a new team of prosecutors to review the evidence and the conduct of the prosecutors. The team discovered that massive amounts of exculpatory evidence had been withheld from the defense and asked Federal District Judge Emmet Sullivan, who presided at the trial, to vacate the verdict and dismiss the indictment.

The department's new investigation was triggered by Judge Sullivan, who throughout the trial had leveled harsh criticism at the conduct of the prosecutors. Judge Sullivan had even held several of the prosecutors in contempt for failing to comply with his discovery orders to disclose exculpatory evidence to the defense. After the indictment was dismissed, Judge Sullivan appointed a special prosecutor, Henry Scheulke, to prosecute the criminal contempt charges. Scheulke conducted a lengthy investigation and issued a 514-page report in which he concluded that the Stevens trial was "permeated" by prosecutorial misconduct, including "the systematic concealment of significant exculpatory evidence which would have independently corroborated Senator Stevens's defense and his testimony, and seriously damaged the testimony and credibility of the government's key witnesses."

Stevens, the powerful Republican senator from Alaska, was indicted for concealing the receipt of $250,000 of free renovation and repair work on his part-time residence in Alaska, and failing to disclose those benefits on his financial disclosure forms that he filed with the senate. The key witness against him was Bill Allen, a businessman and a close friend of Stevens, who made a deal with the prosecutors to testify against Stevens. Allen's cooperation did the renovation work on Stevens's home and according to the government did much of it for free. The critical issue at trial was whether Stevens had a guilty intent when he filed his financial disclosure statements. Stevens claimed he did not intentionally file false statements because he believed that his payment of $160,000 to the contractor covered the entire cost of the renovation. He claimed he did not believe he received any free services from Allen and if he did, then he was not aware of it. However, Stevens's ability to prove his defense was thwarted by the prosecution's concealment of substantial exculpatory evidence and then by preventing attempts by Stevens's lawyers to obtain the evidence. Here are some examples:

Rocky Williams, who supervised the renovation for Allen and was slated to be a key prosecution witness detailing the costs of the renovation and the benefits Stevens received from Allen, told the prosecutors that after reviewing the contractor's bills, it was his understanding that all the renovation costs were correctly billed, that Allen's bills to Stevens reflected the total costs, and that it did not appear that Stevens received any benefits for free. Needless to say, the prosecutors knew that Williams's testimony would corroborate Stevens's defense that he had not knowingly filed false financial forms. Concluding that calling Williams as a witness would damage their case, the prosecutors sent Williams back to Alaska, allegedly for health reasons.

However, the prosecutors never disclosed to the defense Williams's understanding that Stevens received no benefits for free. Moreover, the prosecutors obstructed attempts by the defense to discover this information. Before they sent him back to Alaska they got Williams's assurance that he would not speak to Stevens's lawyers. Moreover, the prosecutors did not memorialize any of Williams's exculpatory statements in any investigative reports which would have been required to be divulged to the defense.

The most egregious suppression of evidence by the prosecutors related to the testimony of Bill Allen. Allen, the prosecution's star witness, testified pursuant to a plea deal that resulted from his participation in a corruption scandal in Alaska. The prosecutors knew from sealed court records that Allen had a sexual relationship with a child prostitute some years earlier after which he directed his lawyers to prepare a false affidavit for the young woman to sign denying that she had sex with Allen. Aware that it would seriously damage Allen's credibility if his sexual relationship was revealed, the prosecutors concealed this evidence from Stevens's lawyers. Thus, since the evidence was under seal, the prosecutors knew that Stevens's lawyers would be unable to discover it on their own. The prosecutors then designed an elaborate scheme to insulate themselves from charges that they violated their disclosure obligations. They consulted with the Justice Department's "ethics advisor" but framed the issue ambiguously: whether or not a person's "recollection" that he may have caused someone to lie needed to be disclosed. Hence, they obtained the answer they wanted as a result of their vagueness. They were assured by this ethics team that they were under no ethical duty to disclose the information.

The prosecutors also were worried that Allen's estimate of the value of the renovations significantly differed from the prosecution's estimate. From the outset, the prosecutors maintained that the value was $250,000, but Allen insisted that the value was no more than $80,000. The prosecutors never disclosed Allen's insistence that the value of the renovations could not have been more than $80,000 to the defense.

The most significant fact supporting Stevens's defense that he intended to pay for all renovation work was evidence that Stevens continued to press Allen to send him bills for all work done. The defense introduced two notes sent by Stevens to Allen in which Stevens expressly requested bills. To the prosecution's chagrin, Allen remembered receiving the notes, but gave various explanations as to why he did not send Stevens any bills. Knowing that the notes would damage their case, perhaps irreparably, and clearly upset by Allen's answers, the prosecutors insinuated to Allen that he was playing games with them and ordered him to "rethink his recollection." After a critical showdown with the prosecutors shortly before the trial, Allen once again was told he better "think a little bit more about what was done," a subtle suggestion that he should alter his testimony.

With the prosecution's case appearing headed for an embarrassing defeat, the prosecutors advised Allen that "he better figure out what he did with the Stevens notes," in effect warning him that he better come up with a persuasive explanation of why he did not send Stevens bills. Suddenly, a few days before the trial, Allen told the prosecutors that he "remembered" a new reason for not sending bills to Stevens; he said he didn't send bills because Stevens told Allen that he made the request for bills just to "cover his ass." This new recollection appeared to save the government's case. However, the prosecutors never disclosed to the defense this new last-minute revelation by Allen.

When Allen testified at trial to this "cover his ass" statement, the defense was stunned; they felt that they were sandbagged. Allen's statement should have been disclosed to the defense before he testified but it was not. The defense asked for an adjournment to deal with this "bombshell." When they cross-examined Allen about when he first concocted the "cover your ass" story, Allen testified that he had told the prosecutors about this statement months earlier in the investigation. But as the prosecutors well knew, this statement by Allen was false. But the prosecutors never corrected it.

The Stevens's prosecutors were not amateurs; they were seasoned veterans, but they conducted themselves with a reckless disregard for the truth and for their constitutional and ethical obligations. When Judge Sullivan ordered them to explain their clear violation of the rules, the prosecutors came up with a variety of excuses. They claimed they were unaware of the existence of exculpatory information; denied that the information was exculpatory; claimed they forgot that the information even existed; claimed they neglected to record certain information; claimed they overlooked the need to scrutinize important source documents; and claimed they were forced by time pressures to do a rushed and unsupervised Brady review and therefore were forced to delegate this task to agents and junior prosecutors who were unfamiliar with the case.

The Sheulke Report describes how the prosecution's conduct with respect to enforcing its Brady obligations was dysfunctional, incompetent, and demonstrated an utter indifference to their duty to serve justice. Indeed, the lead prosecutor represented to the court, falsely, that the government was aware of its Brady obligations and had met them. As noted, the prosecutors delegated to subordinates who lacked experience and close knowledge of the case the task of locating Brady evidence. They were instructed to find evidence that might be "helpful" to the defense, which was not a responsible directive, especially to someone unfamiliar with the case. Also, there were numerous instances when witnesses were interviewed but no official reports were prepared. The conclusion is inescapable that the failure to prepare reports was because such reports would be required to be turned over to the defense. For the same reason, notes were not taken of interviews with witnesses, including interviews in which witnesses like Allen made statements favorable to Stevens.

The prosecutors in other ways deprived the defense of Brady information. Instead of providing the defense with the actual Brady evidence, the prosecutors summarized the evidence broadly to mislead the defense into believing that no Brady evidence existed. Thus, instead of using the actual source documents, the prosecutors used a summary format to discount any "suggestion" that Allen suborned perjury. The source documents would have shown the government's representations to be untrue. Moreover, the prosecutors provided the defense with voluminous electronic documents put into a single-page directory specifically "to make document review more difficult for the defense."

Why did the prosecutors so brazenly break the law, especially under the microscope of such a high-profile case? Did it reflect a "gang" mentality? Perhaps with so many prosecutors involved, each might have believed he or she would be able to deflect responsibility to the other prosecutors. With responsibility thus shared, the prosecutors might have been emboldened to violate the rules with greater impunity. Moreover, with a collective prosecutorial mindset bent on winning a conviction in a high-profile case, there was no one to bring professional training and oversight to bear. Perversely, it may be that prosecutors with such experience may have been in a better position to know how to subvert Brady and game the system.

Two of the federal prosecutors were disciplined by the Justice Department for flagrant misconduct in the Stevens case. They received suspensions of fifteen and forty days. The suspensions were vacated by an administrative judge based on a technical procedural error.

A third prosecutor, Nicholas Marsh, age thirty-seven, committed suicide by hanging himself in his Washington, DC, home after the case began to unravel. His lawyer said Marsh felt burdened by the Stevens prosecution but was confident he would have been exonerated.

Eight days after his conviction, Stevens was narrowly defeated in his bid for reelection. Prior to sentencing, his conviction was dismissed. One year later, Stevens was killed in a plane crash.

"The Thin Blue Line"

When I left the theater after watching the documentary "The Thin Blue Line," I felt shattered. When the film debuted in 1988, the idea that innocent persons were convicted of crimes and imprisoned for years, and maybe executed, had not yet attained its centrality in criminal justice. This extraordinary film depicts the murder of Police Officer Robert Wood in Dallas, Texas, who was shot at point blank range by a motorist he had stopped, who then sped away leaving no clues. After a month-long investigation, Randall Dale Adams was arrested for the murder. His trial, conviction, and death sentence are distilled by chilling interviews of key participants. The film portrays Adams as the victim of a ruthless prosecutor who solicited false testimony to get the conviction. A quote from a local criminal defense attorney resonates throughout the film: "Prosecutors in Dallas have said for years, 'Any prosecutor can convict a guilty man; it takes a great prosecutor to convict an innocent man.'"

Blending monologues, reenactments, old movie clips, visual artifacts, newspaper accounts, maps, drawings, photographs, and police reports, the documentary by Errol Morris meticulously dissects the evidence in the case, reinterviews the key prosecution witnesses, and attempts to ascertain whether Adams is guilty or whether he was framed by the real killer, a young man named David Harris, who was in the car when stopped by Officer Wood. The film's final moment is stunning. We see a tape recorder playing, and hear the voice of Harris and his words superimposed over the machine. Harris, in this "last interview" by Morris, virtually admits that he shot the officer and explains why he framed Adams.

The film suggests, counterintuitively, that a filmmaker's investigation of a murder can be far more reliable than a police investigation, and produce a more just verdict than a jury. In fact, after the film was shown, and based on the film's new revelations, a Texas criminal court held a new hearing in which it found that the trial prosecutor had committed egregious misconduct. The court vacated Adam's conviction and death sentence and ultimately freed him.

We first encounter the prosecutor, Douglas Mulder, known as "Mad Dog" Mulder, as the camera scans a document depicting his victories. We learn that he prosecuted twenty-four death penalty cases, and twenty-four times he won. The film scans a list of the defendants he sent to the state's electric chair. As one of Adam's lawyers notes wryly:

> Douglas Mulder had a perfect win record. I believe he resigned from the D.A.'s office without any defeats. That's why he's legendary. Everything, as I recall, that Mulder ever said was about what a great guy he was, how wonderful it was that he was getting all these convictions.

Harris, the prosecution's star witness, made a deal with Mulder to testify against Adams. The film suggests that Harris, at his young age, could not have been executed, but Adams could be. Harris testified that he was with Adams in the car when Wood stopped the car. According to Harris, the officer walked up to the window and shined his flashlight into the car. Adams then rolled down his window, pulled out a pistol, and "blew the man away." Wood's partner initially gave a description of the shooter, but her description matched Harris, not Adams. Adams testified that he was not in the car, and was nowhere near the location of the shooting. His testimony appeared to be far more believable than Harris's. Adams's lawyers were optimistic that he would be acquitted.

However, the defense was not prepared for Mulder's rebuttal case. He sandbagged the defense. Without prior notice, he called several new witnesses whose testimony doomed Adams. The most devastating witness was Emily Miller. We see an artist's rendition of Miller on the witness stand as we hear Adams's lawyer describing the key moment in the trial when Miller waved her finger at Adams and declared, "That's the man! I saw that man! I saw Randall Adams' face. I saw the gun sticking out of the car when he shot that police officer, and that's the man." Miller got Adams convicted.

The filmmaker's posttrial interview of Emily Miller is devastating. Watching it, there is a certainty that her courtroom testimony was false. Her free-flowing monologue on camera has a stunning, almost surreal impact, far different from the rigid question and answer style of trial testimony. Smiling, smirking, and self-absorbed, Miller seems to be infatuated by her moment on camera and appears to crave the limelight. She describes how she loves detective stories like Boston Blackie, and how "everywhere I go there are murders, even around my house." Her explanation of how she was able to make an identification of the shooter from her car, at night, at a considerable distance, with the windows closed, appears absurd, even comical. Her rambling narrative obliterates any pretense that her in-court identification of Adams was reliable and truthful.

The film goes on to reveal unsettling information about Miller which neither the jury nor Adams' lawyers knew about. We learn that Miller became a prosecution witness only after she was arrested for disorderly and violent behavior and saw a chance to make a deal; she viewed a line-up and picked out someone other than Adams; she identified Adams only after a police officer pointed out Adams as the murderer; she knew about and sought the large reward for information about the killing; her daughter was about to stand trial for armed robbery carrying a sentence of life imprisonment but a week after Miller testified, the charges against her daughter were dropped; Miller was fired from her job at a gas station two weeks before her testimony for stealing from her boss and according to a fellow employee, "Miller never told the truth in her life."

The jury's decision to execute Adams resulted from the testimony of the prosecutor's expert, Dr. James P. Grigson, famously known as "Dr. Death." Grigson told the jury that Adams was a psychopath and degenerate killer who would kill again if kept alive.

Adams was three days from being executed when a court stayed his execution. Thereafter, a Texas appeals court vacated his conviction based on Mulder's misconduct, particularly his suppression of the evidence that discredited Emily Miller as well as knowingly allowing Miller to lie. Mulder's misconduct was compounded, according to the appeals court, when, after the defense was alerted that Emily Miller may have committed perjury and wanted to have her recalled, Mulder told the court, untruthfully, that Miller had left the jurisdiction and he did not know her present whereabouts.

David Harris was never tried for the Wood murder. He was tried and convicted for a different murder, and executed.

Dr. Grigson was expelled from the American Psychiatric Association and the Texas Psychiatric Association for ethical violations.

After watching the film I wrote to Adams. "I am sure of my cause," he wrote back. He asked me "to give a special prayer when you hear news of my cause in the future." "But," he added, "who knows what the future holds."

After his release and exoneration, Adams became an anti-death penalty activist. He died on October 30, 2010, of a brain tumor at the age of sixty-one.

Chapter Seven

Conflicts

The Problem of Divided Loyalties

Prosecutors occasionally face situations that present the potential for conflicts of interest. A prosecutor previously may have participated in a case as a private attorney and acquired information that could be used against persons involved in the private litigation, even against a former client. Or, given the fact that most state and local prosecutors are elected, there is always the temptation for a prosecutor to use his office to advance his political or personal interests. Rules about ethics try to regulate conflicts, but many prosecutors evade or ignore such restrictions.

In some cases, the conflict between a prosecutor's impartial service to justice and his self-serving conduct may be so egregious as to suggest bad faith. Examples abound: in one well-known case, New Orleans district attorney James Garrison decided to investigate the assassination of President Kennedy ostensibly because Lee Harvey Oswald had spent the summer of 1963 in New Orleans. Garrison focused his investigation on a businessman named Clay Shaw after the release of the Warren Commission Report in 1966. In 1967, Garrison charged Shaw with conspiring to assassinate Kennedy. Although Shaw was tried and acquitted, Garrison recharged him with perjury based on his testimony at his trial. A federal court took the extraordinary step of enjoining the state prosecution, finding that it was brought in bad faith and for venal motives. One of these motives, the court found, was Garrison's desire to gain financially from his forthcoming book on the Kennedy assassination, which would be promoted by the publicity surrounding the Shaw prosecutions.

A more recent case of bad faith prosecution was the conduct of former Arizona prosecutor Andrew Thomas, who was disbarred by a state ethics commission for violating the public trust by engaging in repeated conflicts of interest. Thomas, it was found, conducted a personal vendetta against judges, lawmakers, lawyers, and others who opposed him politically. He convened a grand jury and indicted these individuals for felonies based on virtually no evidence. All of the charges were ultimately dismissed. Thomas's alliance with notorious Maricopa County Sheriff Joe Arpaio helped Thomas bring the malicious and unfounded criminal charges. According to the state disciplinary panel, Thomas "dishonored, desecrated, and defiled the public trust."

The following stories describe other types of conflicts by prosecutors. For some prosecutors, avenging the harm to victims is the highest priority, but can a prosecutor's overzealous commitment to a victim create a conflict by distorting the prosecutor's objectivity and impartiality when examining the evidence and possibly ignoring or minimizing evidence that might suggest that the person whom the victim accused is really innocent? Also, what is the duty of a prosecutor who believes a defendant is innocent but has been directed to prosecute the case? Should he simply remove himself from the case, or should he take some affirmative act to protect the defendant from a wrongful conviction? Finally, because of the close working relationship between prosecutors and police, is there an institutional conflict for a prosecutor when presented with evidence of criminal behavior by the police? In such cases, should an independent special prosecutor who has no connection to the police under investigation be appointed?

Prosecutor as Victim's Surrogate

Bobby Franklin was an assistant district attorney in Howard County, Tennessee. He prosecuted Danny Whitehead for the murder of Sheila Towns, Whitehead's girlfriend. The trial ended in a hung jury. Several months after the trial, Franklin left the district attorney's office and went into private practice. When the case against Whitehead was tried a second time, Towns's family decided to hire a private lawyer to serve as cocounsel with Sherman Davis, the new assistant district attorney trying the case. The family decided to retain Bobby Franklin. The retention of

Franklin was authorized by a state law that allows a victim or a victim's family to hire private legal counsel to assist the prosecution and participate in the trial subject to the prosecutor's discretion.

The family's decision to hire Franklin to assist Davis made sense. Davis was a relative newcomer to prosecution. In fact, Franklin handled most of the prosecution, examining and cross-examining key witnesses, and making the opening and closing arguments to the jury. Whitehead was convicted of murder and sentenced to life in prison.

One month after Whitehead's conviction, Davis resigned from the district attorney's office and entered private practice with Franklin. The two lawyers then filed a civil wrongful death action on behalf of Towns's family against Whitehead and won a substantial monetary judgment.

This story raises significant conflicts of interest by prosecutors. Does the close involvement by a private lawyer in the prosecution of a case—indeed, as a surrogate prosecutor on behalf of the victim—violate any ethics rules of professional conduct? Although this practice appears to be unusual, it is not uncommon. Many states follow the common law tradition of allowing victims to hire private attorneys to assist the prosecution, and even to prosecute the case themselves. However, the risk of an ethical conflict from this practice is obvious. Indeed, the potential for such a conflict led the U.S. Supreme Court to establish a categorical rule in the federal courts against the practice of a judge appointing a private attorney for an interested party in order to bring a contempt action for that private party alleging a violation of a court order. Recognizing the fundamental premise that a prosecutor must wield the formidable powers of the criminal law in a rigorously disinterested fashion to serve the cause of justice exclusively, the court held that the appointment of a prosecutor with a special interest to a private client rather than the cause of justice creates an appearance of impropriety that diminishes public confidence in the criminal justice system.

Applying the Supreme Court's reasoning, did the retention of a private attorney by the Towns family to assist the prosecution of the Whitehead murder case compromise, at least from an ethical standpoint, the integrity of the trial? Furthermore, even if no ethical conflict existed, did the conduct of the prosecution in allowing a private attorney to participate in the proceedings in such a substantial way impair the fairness of the trial as a matter of constitutional due process?

The Whitehead case clearly shows the potential for an ethical conflict when a private prosecutor hired by the victim or the victim's family assists the prosecution. Such representation has the potential to undermine the integrity of the prosecution by placing the prosecutor in a situation where he is required to serve two masters, namely, the victim and the cause of justice. Whether the victim actually influenced the actions of the prosecution may not be clear, but there is certainly the appearance that the victim influenced the prosecution for private interests unrelated to the public interest. That appearance may be sufficient to compromise the integrity of the trial from an ethical standpoint.

What are the possible ways that the private prosecutor in the above case may have compromised the cause of justice? Since a private prosecutor's ethical duty is to his client, it is unlikely that the prosecution would accept a guilty plea from the defendant if the victim opposed the deal. Similarly, it is questionable whether the prosecution would readily disclose discovery material or exculpatory evidence to the defendant as required by law. Moreover, as shown in the above case, it is likely that the victim probably influenced the prosecutor's exercise of official discretion by the attorney's subsequent private practice affiliation and the bringing of a civil lawsuit against the defendant.

The case also illustrates the increased role of crime victims today, and the close relationship between crime victims and prosecutors. Crime victims today are afforded broad legal protections. Every state and the federal government have statutes affording crime victims numerous protections, including a right to be treated fairly and with dignity, a right to restitution for their injuries, a right to be protected from the accused, a right to be notified and be present at court proceedings, and a right to be heard at critical stages of the proceedings. These protections naturally require the involvement and cooperation of the prosecutor.

The relationship between prosecutors and crime victims has always been close, cooperative, and mutually reinforcing.

For any prosecutor, crimes involving victims, especially crimes of physical violence, abuse of vulnerable persons, and invasions of personal and property rights, understandably invite a sympathetic response and a demand for justice. Also, crimes against victims generally produce indisputable evidence of an invasive act allowing a prosecutor to present a compelling account of guilt through the victim that will be readily believed by a jury. Moreover, the prosecutor, through skillful use of evidence and argument, is able to exploit a jury's natural inclination to empathize with the victim and invite revenge. Finally, since the issue before a jury is the victim's accuracy rather than his or her truthfulness, a prosecutor will usually be more successful in persuading the jury to accept the testimony of an honest but mistaken victim than the self-serving testimony of an unsavory witness with a strong motivation to lie, such as an accomplice or an informant.

Although the conduct of the attorneys in the above case appears to violate ethical rules, it does not follow that the conduct compromises the fairness of the trial as a matter of constitutional due process. Here it would be necessary to determine whether the private prosecutor has a personal or financial interest in the outcome of the case, whether the assistant district attorney maintained control and management over the prosecution or delegated significant functions to the private attorney, and whether the assistant district attorney had an interest in any pending civil action concerning the same facts as the criminal case.

In the case above, there is no indication that the private attorney was involved in civil litigation on behalf of the victim's family at the time of the criminal prosecution, nor is there any indication that the actual prosecutor, despite ceding extensive prosecutorial authority to the private prosecutor, did not retain control of the prosecution and the various discretionary decisions needed to be made. There is no indication of any actual misconduct by the assistant district attorney or the private prosecutor that prejudiced the defendant's right to a fair trial. However, it does appear likely that the prosecution was intended to further a private agenda, especially in view of the subsequent affiliation between the assistant district attorney and the private prosecutor, and their joint representation of the victim's family in the civil action against the defendant.

There are other opportunities for conflicts that result from a prosecutor's simultaneous representation of a private client, as would be the case when a prosecutor is employed part-time pursuant to state or local law, as are many prosecutors. Indeed, one-fourth of all prosecutors in state courts in the United States are employed part-time. There is obviously the risk that a part-time prosecutor might become involved in private matters that might relate to official matters.

For example, in *Ganger v. Peyton*, a part-time prosecutor represented a wife in a divorce action which was precipitated by an assault on her by her husband. While representing the wife, the prosecutor initiated a prosecution against the husband for assault. The prosecutor offered to drop the assault charge if the defendant's husband made a divorce settlement favorable to the wife. Because of the prosecutor's own self-interest in the civil litigation, including the possibility that the size of his fee might be contingent on what he could exact from the husband-defendant, the prosecutor was not able to exercise fair-minded judgment about whether to decline prosecution, reduce the charge, or recommend a suspended sentence or other clemency. The prosecutor in such case could not serve two masters and therefore, as the court found, he violated due process.

Serving a Client or One's Conscience?

On Thanksgiving night in 1990, at around 1 a.m. outside the Palladium nightclub in downtown Manhattan, while revelers inside were celebrating "Latin Night," a fight erupted near the front entrance ropes. Witnesses saw a Hispanic man get into a fight with a bouncer. The man left but returned moments later with friends carrying guns. Shots were fired at close range and two bouncers were hit. Markus Peterson, twenty-three, an amateur bodybuilder from Brooklyn, was shot in the chest and died hours later on a hospital operating table. Jeff Craig, a retired New York City police officer, was shot in the thigh and survived.

Several weeks later, David Lemus, a twenty-two-year-old construction worker who was also attending night school to become a carpenter's apprentice, was picked out of a photo array as the shooter. A month later, he was picked out in a lineup, arrested, and charged with the murder of Peterson and attempted murder of Craig. Ten months later, Olmedo Hidalgo, a twenty-six-year-old immigrant from the Dominican Republic who was working at his brother's grocery store was also identified from photos and a lineup and charged as well. Lemus and Hidalgo had previous arrests, Lemus for gun possession and Hidalgo for driving a stolen car.

Two years after the shooting, Lemus and Hidalgo went to trial together in Manhattan Supreme Court. The prosecution's case was strong. Four witnesses positively identified Lemus and Hidalgo as the shooters. All four said the area was well-lit and that they got a good look at the persons who did it. Another witness, Delores Spencer, Lemus's ex-girlfriend, testified that Lemus told her a few days after the shooting that he was one of the gunmen. Although he later told her that he had made up the story to impress her, this later statement was kept from the jury. The defense called no witnesses.

On December 2, 1992, Lemus and Hidalgo were found guilty of murder and attempted murder and sentenced to twenty-five years to life in prison.

However, the Palladium case did not go away with the jury's verdict. It became one of New York's most high-profile cases raising the claim that the defendants were innocent. One person who became obsessed with the case was Bronx homicide detective Bobby Addorato, who had been involved in the initial investigation. He once said that of all the cases he handled, the Palladium case was the one case that kept him up at night. He recalled that a few years after the Palladium trial, he heard from an informant who said he had been sitting in his parked car at the nightclub and saw the shooting. According to the informant, two of his fellow gang members, Joey Pilot and Spanky Morales, gunned down the bouncers. Afterward, while working with federal prosecutors investigating gang activity, Addorato arrested Pilot and Morales. Pilot, looking to cut a deal, told the prosecutors that Morales shot the bouncers and that he, Pilot, had fired too, but that his nine-millimeter gun jammed and an unfired bullet fell to the ground. Police reports had noted that an unfired nine-millimeter cartridge was found at the scene. Probing further, Addorato noticed in the files that a few days after the shooting an anonymous tipster had called Crime Stoppers and identified Pilot and Morales as the gunmen. Addorato also located three witnesses who claimed that Morales bragged about the killing. Although this new evidence raised enough doubts about the guilt of Lemus and Hidalgo to warrant a court hearing in 1995, the prosecutors insisted that the right men had been convicted and the judge agreed, finding Pilot's story "entirely unworthy of belief."

Over the next few years, more evidence was uncovered that further undermined confidence in the verdicts. Prosecutors discovered that two witnesses had identified Morales as the shooter but that he had never been placed in a lineup. Also, there was a note in the police file that Morales's sister-in-law had called police in 1991 reporting that Morales was involved in the shooting. *The New York Times* also weighed in with an editorial in 2000 critical of the justice of the Palladium convictions. After reading the editorial, an inmate in federal prison told prosecutors that he was with Morales the night of the murder, that he saw Morales shoot the bouncers, and that neither Lemus nor Hidalgo was involved. Under intense public pressure and facing increasing doubts about the reliability of the verdicts, Manhattan district attorney Robert Morgenthau agreed to take a fresh look at the case. He tasked one of his senior assistants, Daniel Bibb, to lead the re-examination.

Bibb was the right person for the job. He was a career prosecutor with no partisan agenda, totally honest, and claimed he never prejudged the merits of cases he handled. Bibb looked the part. Tall, square-jawed, with a resonant voice, he was tough, fair, and totally dedicated to serving the cause of justice. He had handled many of the most important murder cases in the office and many cold-case investigations too. His impartiality and sound judgment were widely respected. People knew that if Bibb had doubts about the guilt of someone he was prosecuting, he would struggle to resolve those doubts before going ahead with the prosecution. As he began to reinvestigate the Palladium case he admitted "it was the most difficult case I'd ever had."

Bibb was given carte blanche by his superiors to get to the truth. He was told to leave no stone unturned. His investigation lasted nearly two years. He and two detectives conducted more than fifty interviews in over a dozen states. They located numerous witnesses that the police had never before interviewed. As Bibb got deeper into the case, his doubts about the defendants' guilt continued to grow. At a critical meeting with his superiors in 2005, after the court had granted a motion by the defense lawyers for a new hearing, Bibb urged that the convictions be set aside. He made a powerful presentation of the facts to show that the defendants were not involved in the shooting, but his superiors did not agree to drop the cases. They ordered him to go to the hearing, present the prosecution's best case, and let the judge decide. To Bibb, this was an utterly irresponsible decision. If he didn't believe in his case, how could he prosecute it responsibly? Bibb faced a torturous decision. He knew that if he withdrew from the case some other prosecutor would take over and possibly win it. What was Bibb to do?

He decided to go into court and represent his office, but he planned to do everything he could to lose the case. To accomplish that result, he decided to secretly contact the defense lawyers and familiarize them with the new evidence he uncovered and help them present this evidence effectively. In long phone conversations, he acquainted the lawyers with his proof; helped them interpret the proof; identified which witnesses they should call; helped locate the witnesses in prison or in witness protection programs; when necessary help them persuade the witnesses to testify; help them prepare the testimony to have its greatest impact; did not object during their cross-examination; and, during court breaks, advised the lawyers where he felt they were not asking the right questions. "I'm your best friend in that courtroom," he told them. When the hearing was over, he made one final pitch with his superiors. They agreed to drop the case against Hidalgo but refused to dismiss Lemus. "I'm done," Bibb recalled. "I wanted nothing more to do with it."

In October 2005, the court vacated Lemus's conviction and ordered a new trial. Lemus was released from prison after fourteen years. Bibb resigned a few months later. After a retrial in 2007, with new identification witnesses testifying that Lemus was not involved in the shooting, Lemus was found not guilty.

When the story of Bibb's conduct in helping the defense became public, the focus naturally centered on the ethical questions involved: had Bibb violated a rule of professional ethics by betraying his client, the district attorney, and by secretly assisting defense lawyers to win the case? Did the district attorney subvert the cause of justice by ordering an assistant to prosecute a case in which there were strong grounds to believe that the defendants were innocent? District Attorney Morgenthau made a public statement defending his office's conduct. He asserted that Bibb was never asked to prosecute someone he believed to be innocent. According to Morgenthau, Bibb was asked only to participate in a fact-finding hearing to determine the position his office should take with respect to the murder convictions.

Morgenthau noted that following the hearing, his office agreed to dismiss one of the convictions and prosecute the second defendant at a retrial based on the testimony of several eyewitnesses who confirmed his guilt.

Academics weighed in on both sides of the ethics debate. On one side, Bibb was accused of violating his obligation to his client. According to this view, although a lawyer certainly is entitled to his conscience and to make decisions in accordance with his conscientiously held beliefs, he is not entitled to subvert his client's case. He must either withdraw from the case or resign. Under a different view, however, a prosecutor is not only an adversary, he is also a minister of justice whose duty is to seek not victory but justice.

Bibb was actually brought before a bar disciplinary agency and investigated for his conduct in the Palladium case. He defended himself. Following its investigation, the agency informed Bibb that it saw no basis for disciplinary action and closed its inquiry.

Bibb always imagined himself as a prosecutor for his entire professional career. He was an outstanding prosecutor, but he paid a heavy price for doing what he and many observers believe was the right thing.

Bibb resigned from the district attorney's office after Morgenthau decided to retry Lemus. He is presently in private practice and represents clients in New York and New Jersey. For Bibb, life is good, but the Palladium case is never far from his mind.

Prosecutor-Police Alliance

After six years in the Manhattan District Attorney's Office, I accepted a position with the Office of the Deputy Attorney General charged with investigating corruption in New York City's criminal justice system. The office was created by New York's Governor Nelson Rockefeller after extensive hearings in 1971 by the "Knapp Commission" into police corruption. In fact, the commission revealed widespread corruption by police and other government officials, which the local district attorneys—including the district attorney's office in which I was serving—either ignored or failed to investigate properly. The theory behind the creation of this new "special prosecutor's office" was that given the close structural ties between prosecutors and police, it is difficult for prosecutors to maintain an independent and impartial attitude toward police corruption and misconduct. Needless to say, the local prosecutors did not agree. They did not believe that they were unable to investigate the police and claimed that the new special prosecutor's office was not only unnecessary but also a tacit slight to the effectiveness and integrity of the district attorneys.

When I told Manhattan district attorney Frank S. Hogan, one of the nations most distinguished prosecutors, that I was planning to accept a position with the new special prosecutor, Maurice Nadjari, I did not expect Mr. Hogan's response. When I told him I wanted to finish up my work, and that I would remain until then, he looked at me coldly and replied, "No, you'll leave today." Nadjari's office, he asserted, was a blot on the reputation and honor of every district attorney in the city, that I was disloyal, and unworthy of remaining another day. I left his office stunned. I cleaned out my office that day, and departed 155 Leonard Street (subsequently renamed "Hogan Plaza") for the last time.

Internal Investigations of Police Shootings of Unarmed Civilians

Was Mr. Hogan correct? Or are there special bonds between prosecutors and police that make investigations of police by special prosecutors necessary? In Chapter 2, which recounts stories about the work of prosecutors in grand juries, I discuss two troubling cases in which prosecutors appeared to go out of their ways to exonerate police officers accused of killing unarmed civilians. Another example of why local prosecutors cannot be trusted to investigate unlawful conduct by police is the action of Rensselaer County district attorney Joel Abelove. Abelove defied an Executive Order from New York's Governor Andrew Cuomo which designated Attorney General Eric Schneiderman as special prosecutor to investigate police shootings of unarmed civilians. Despite repeated requests from Schneiderman to turn over his investigative files of a highly publicized police shooting, Abelove refused to turn over the files, told the media that Schneiderman's office would not be in charge of the investigation, rushed the case into his own grand jury, gave the police officer who fired the fatal shots immunity, did not call two civilian witnesses who saw the shooting and who disputed the officer's account, and then got the grand jury to clear the officer.

Abelove's conduct dramatically illustrates how prosecutors and police can work together to protect each other's interests and by covering for each other, undermine the public's interest in the fair and evenhanded enforcement of law.

The tragic death of Edson Thevenin, a thirty-seven-year-old African-American, began in the early hours of April 17 in Troy, New York, when he was pulled over by Police Sgt. Randy French for allegedly driving while intoxicated. The police version alleged that Thevenin fled in his vehicle, was chased by police cruisers, that during the chase Thevenin's car struck French, and that French then shot him eight times through the windshield, striking him four times in the head, and four times in his body. Thevenin was unarmed. French claimed he suffered minor leg injuries in the encounter. Thevenin's wife said that a police detective told her that her husband died in a car accident.

The day after Thevenin was killed, District Attorney Abelove stood next to the Troy police chief during a press conference in which the chief defended his cops. As he told the media: "We are fully supporting Sgt. French and his actions. It would appear that the actions of Sgt. French are certainly in line with the law enforcement policy and training."

However, pursuant to the Governor's Executive Order, Schneiderman's office immediately got involved in the shooting. Schneiderman's investigators went to the scene of the shooting but were rebuffed by the police. The following day, Schneiderman informed Abelove that the state attorney general's office, in line with the Governor's Executive Order, was reviewing the case, and directed Abelove to take no action pending Schneiderman's review. Schneiderman sent Abelove a letter requesting the files. Notwithstanding Schneiderman's explicit and repeated directives and requests, Abelove quickly empaneled a grand jury, called only two police witnesses, gave them immunity, and gave the grand jury legal instructions that in effect directed the grand jury to clear the officer.

Schneiderman then brought an extraordinary lawsuit against Abelove to invalidate Abelove's unlawful conduct. According to Schneiderman's court papers, Abelove flagrantly violated the Governor's Executive Order, took actions that "flew in the face of the public concerns," effectively snuck the case through the grand jury without notifying Schneiderman's office, and presented the case in such a partisan, police-friendly manner as to undermine the integrity of the grand jury process. Moreover, as the lawsuit notes, Abelove was hardly a fair and impartial prosecutor sworn to uphold the cause of justice. He appeared to have acted in bad faith and abused his authority. This was the first time a local district attorney attempted to violate the Governor's

Executive Order. However, Abelove's conduct was not surprising. He had earlier mocked the concept of a special prosecutor, telling a local newspaper that he had "grave concerns" over the governor's order, that the order was confusing and contradictory, and that he would not succumb to a "vocal minority" by refraining from prosecuting police shootings of civilians.

There is no rational explanation for Abelove's granting immunity to Sgt. French and thereby protecting French from criminal liability in fatally shooting Thevenin. There is no rational explanation for Abelove calling into the grand jury only the two police witnesses and not calling the two civilians who apparently witnessed the entire incident and gave written statements to the police. Both witnesses told investigators that they did not believe Sgt. French was in imminent danger when he fired the eight shots through Thevenin's windshield. One of these witnesses allegedly took a cellphone video of at least part of the incident and claimed that French opened fire before the car struck French. Of course, if French shot and killed the motorist before the car lurched forward at French, it is hardly a surprise that the car, now driven by a dead motorist, may have been out of control.

Faced with the lawsuit, Abelove finally agreed to turn over his files to Schneiderman in return for Schneiderman dropping the lawsuit. Schneiderman, however, said he would continue to look into Abelove's conduct and that he was not "off the hook" for his unlawful actions. Since disciplinary proceedings are confidential, it is not known if Abelove is being investigated by New York's disciplinary agency for his willful defiance. Indeed, Abelove, recently elected, has quickly come under ethical scrutiny for conflicts of interest in other cases: first, in a case involving a political crony in which he should have disqualified himself, and second, in a case involving a fellow Republican politician charged with embezzlement. His present conduct in flouting the governor's order and then secretly undermining the attorney general's investigation almost certainly involves misconduct in violation of Rule 8.4 of the rules of professional conduct which prohibits all lawyers, including prosecutors, from "engaging in conduct that is prejudicial to the administration of justice." It is hard to imagine a stronger case of a prosecutor engaging in conduct that undermines the administration of justice than a prosecutor deliberately violating a lawful order of a government official.

Interestingly, a recent report commissioned by New York State's chief judge on attorney discipline in New York State felt it was unnecessary to create a special disciplinary body to investigate misconduct by prosecutors. According to the report, "The Commission has no reason to doubt that the grievance and disciplinary committees diligently examine claims of prosecutorial misconduct that come to their attention." Abelove's misconduct has certainly come to the attention of the disciplinary authorities. Whether the public should have confidence that "the disciplinary system is doing its job and the system is working" may be open to doubt.

Systematic Violation of Defendants' Rights by Orange County California Prosecutors and Sheriff's Office

Another egregious instance of the unholy relationship between prosecutors and police is currently roiling the Orange County, California, criminal justice system. The story begins with the massacre at the Salon Meritage hair salon in Seal Beach, California, in October, 2011, in which Scott Dekraai walked into the salon and shot eight people to death. Dekraai was involved in a custody dispute with his wife, one of the victims. Dekraai pleaded guilty and the proceeding to seek his death sentence was about to start when his lawyer made a stunning revelation to the court: for years, the Orange County Sheriff's Department and the Orange County District Attorney's Office had been engaged in a systematic effort to violate the constitutional rights of defendants by deliberately placing informants in their cells pretending to be friends to gain their confidence and then, in violation of their Sixth Amendment right to counsel, to secretly record incriminating conversations with them. One of the targets secretly taped was Dekraai. The police-prosecution team's conduct may have placed hundreds of other criminal cases in jeopardy.

When Judge Thomas Goethals was asked by Dekraai's lawyer to order the prosecutors to produce records of the jailhouse informant program, the judge was hardly aware of the titanic convulsions that would ensue. He was appalled to learn that over 5,000 pages of police documents existed for only one of the informants, which appeared to jeopardize nine cases, including Dekraai's. As Judge Goethals got deeper into the cases, he discovered that prosecutors, in collusion with the sheriff's department, had deliberately suppressed critical exculpatory information from defense lawyers that would have destroyed the credibility of the police informants. It appeared that prosecutors were so desperately bent on winning convictions that they violated clearly established law.

Judge Goethals heard testimony for almost a year, including testimony from twenty-eight prosecutors who claimed that their improper conduct was not intentional, and that it resulted from heavy caseloads, miscommunication, and inadvertent errors. Judge Goethals was unable to find sufficient systemic corruption between prosecutors and police to taint any of the cases. He did bar the prosecutors from using at Dekraai's sentencing hearing any of Dekraai's statements made to jailhouse informants.

But after digging further, Dekraai's lawyer found the proverbial "smoking gun"; records suggesting that the sheriff's department, in collusion with the prosecutors, deliberately placed informants into specially selected cells with the explicit purpose to promote secret taping of conversations with these selected inmates. Based on this new disclosure, Judge Goethals reopened the hearing. He was so disturbed by the new evidence showing what he called the prosecution's "serious, ongoing discovery violations" that he disqualified every member of the Orange County District Attorney's Office from the prosecution of Dekraai. He faulted the district attorney, Tony Rackauckas, for acting in tandem with the sheriff's department in flagrantly violating the defendant's rights.

The Orange County criminal justice system may be on the verge of collapse. Dozens of serious felony cases have been affected by the revelations; sheriff's deputies are refusing to testify in cases by invoking their Fifth Amendment rights; a local defense attorney was beaten up by one of the district attorney's investigators; prosecutors continue to take a cavalier and flippant attitude that they did nothing wrong except for a few honest mistakes; prosecutors have sought to disqualify Judge Goethals from virtually every case based on his alleged bias against them; and numerous persons joined in a letter asking the U.S. Justice Department to conduct a civil rights investigation of Orange County.

California's attorney general appealed Judge Goethals's disqualification of the district attorney's office, arguing that no conflict existed. In unanimously affirming Judge Geothals' order, the appellate court strongly disagreed with the attorney general, finding that the district attorney "had an actual conflict because loyalty to the sheriff's department prevented the district attorney from performing its constitutional and statutory obligations." The appellate court found that the prosecutors had "intentionally or negligently ignored the sheriff's department's violations of targeted defendants' constitutional rights but on its own violated targeted defendants' constitutional rights."

The U.S. Department of Justice has opened a civil rights investigation into the Orange County District Attorney's Office and sheriff's department over allegations that both agencies violated the rights of numerous defendants through the tainted jailhouse informant program. According to the head of the department's Civil Rights Division, "A systematic failure to protect the right to counsel and to a fair trial makes criminal proceedings fundamentally unfair and diminishes the public's faith in the integrity of the justice system."

Improper Prosecutor-Judge Relations— Sleeping with a Judge?

What could be more grotesque for a defendant being tried for capital murder and facing execution than a trial in which the judge and prosecutor are having a secret sexual relationship and, working in tandem, cause a defendant to be found guilty of murder and face execution? That incredible scenario appears to have happened to Charles Hood. On trial for murder in a Texas courtroom, Hood claimed, correctly as it turns out, that the judge and the prosecutor were having a sexual relationship during his trial and that his right to a fair trial was thereby compromised. A lower court agreed to the extent of ordering a hearing, but the highest appeals court in Texas reversed this decision. Why? Not because they discounted Hood's claim on the merits. They dismissed his complaint on a procedural technicality; Hood failed to raise the claim in earlier pleadings. According to the Texas appeals court, since Hood was unable to substantiate the "rumors" of the affair with sufficient proof during his trial, he was procedurally barred from raising the claim after the trial was over. The Texas prosecutor, with a straight face, hailed the decision "as a significant procedural victory."

It is hard to imagine a sleazier and more dangerous conflict for a prosecutor and a judge than one in which the two are having an affair during a capital murder trial.

Interestingly, the prosecutor in Hood's trial did not say that the defendant's allegation lacked merit; the prosecutor knew otherwise. Indeed, the judge and the trial prosecutor—a different prosecutor from the appeals prosecutor—acknowledged the love affair in sworn depositions taken after Hood's trial. The prosecutor did not claim that Hood was not prejudiced, or that justice was served, which of course is the legal and ethical mandate of every prosecutor. The prosecutor could not say this, of course, because Hood's right to a fair trial was almost certainly prejudiced by the affair. If the prosecutor believed that the pursuit of justice was his mission, as it is for every prosecutor, at the very least he should have agreed before the appeals court that a hearing was necessary, as the lower court had ordered. The appeals prosecutor did not appear to be troubled by the fact that that the trial judge was later elevated to the same appeals court, and she sat with many of the same judges who denied Hood the opportunity to prove his innocence.

Leaving aside for the moment the ugliness of a prosecutor and judge having a love affair during a capital murder trial, one of the most nefarious games that prosecutors play is to aggressively raise hypertechnical and attenuated procedural obstacles that a defendant must overcome in order to get a court to listen to his often meritorious claim that the prosecutor committed misconduct. Indeed, the Supreme Court has characterized such prosecutorial conduct as "gambling" and "playing the odds" with a defendant's rights, and playing "hide and seek" to avoid disclosure of exonerating evidence, and requiring a defendant to engage in "scavenger hunts" to find exonerating evidence of which the prosecutor is secretly aware, but has suppressed.

Thus, even if a prosecutor knows full well that a defendant's claim is legitimate and meritorious, prosecutors regularly argue that the defendant should not be allowed to raise it because he failed to raise his claim earlier, as with Hood, even though the prosecutor knew full well that the defendant could not raise the claim earlier because he did not have the information which, brazenly, the prosecutor had suppressed. Some prosecutors have even sought to deflect a defendant's postconviction claim of innocence by arguing that the defendant pleaded the wrong theory, or failed to use the correct nomenclature to describe the violation. Too many courts have endorsed such irresponsible prosecutorial arguments. A few years ago, in *Banks v. Dretke*, the Supreme Court slapped down the prosecutor for, among other procedural ploys, arguing that the defendant, in effect, "Didn't say Simon Sez" by failing to differentiate clearly enough between his distinct legal claims.

Procedural gamesmanship by prosecutors is not a new phenomenon. But with the increasing demands by courts for enhanced and much more rigorous pleading requirements, defendants like Charles Hood are going to find the gateway to justice littered with procedural hoops and mazes of sufficient magnitude and complexity that a defendant may be barred from establishing the merits of his or her claim that the prosecutor engaged in shocking misconduct, like sleeping with the judge, that denied him a fair trial. Some prosecutors, like the prosecutor of Charles Hood, who sent Hood to the death chamber, will champion this result as a major victory.

Chapter Eight

Fighting Corruption

Are Corruption Prosecutions Different?

I served in the special prosecutor's office charged with investigating and prosecuting corruption in New York City. The media glamorized the office right at its inception in 1972. Corruption was a big public concern, underscored by the sensational cases of police corruption exposed by the "Knapp Commission," created by New York's mayor to investigate widespread allegations of corruption by police, judges, and lawyers in the city's criminal justice system. My office won almost all of our prosecution cases against corrupt cops. However, when we began to prosecute corruption by judges and other high government officials, we encountered resistance in the appellate courts which questioned our investigative methods and often found we had overreached. In one highly publicized case, we used a sham arrest and phony prosecution that led to the indictment of several judges and lawyers. To pretend the case was real, we had to create fictitious court documents and present fictitious testimony before the grand jury. Judges found our tactics shocking and threw out indictments. The media turned on us, our office's reputation was diminished, and the office was ultimately terminated.

Prosecuting corruption crimes is challenging. There are significant differences between prosecuting crimes of violence and prosecuting crimes of corruption, From the prosecutor's standpoint, crimes of violence typically have victims who complain, whereas crimes of corruption are typically committed in secret, with the consent of the participants, and without a complainant. Moreover, crimes of violence generally have direct and often tangible evidence of the crime—eyewitnesses, weapons, and forensic evidence. Corruption crimes usually have no witnesses who are willing to come forward and no tangible evidence; the prosecutor must rely on the testimony of accomplices who agree to cooperate with the government, or possibly informants or undercover agents pretending to be criminals who have been invited into the corrupt scheme. Finally, with crimes of violence, there is usually no question of the honesty of the victim; a conviction typically hinges on the victim's reliability. Convictions for corruption, by contrast, almost always hinge on the truthfulness of government witnesses and where possible, the acquisition of incriminating statements through the use of electronic evidence—wiretaps, consensual recordings, and surveillance videos.

Moreover, with crimes of violence, a prosecutor is often able to present to juries a much more dramatic and compelling story than with corruption crimes. With a violent crime, there is a victim and witnesses whom the jury can see and empathize with. There are typically no suggestions that the prosecutor has a personal or political interest in winning the case, as there might be when prosecuting political crimes, white-collar crimes, and official corruption. Political considerations may invite prosecutorial abuse, as was the case during the Bush Administration's firing of several U.S. attorneys and then launching what appeared to be political investigations of corruption and voter fraud. The frequent calls for the appointment of special prosecutors to investigate official misconduct and political corruption suggests that at least from the standpoint of the public, the appointment of an independent, nonpolitical investigator is the ideal recourse to avoid claims of a political coverup.

I wondered (and still wonder) if there should be different institutional and ethical standards for prosecutors when investigating and prosecuting crimes of corruption and crimes of violence. How much should a prosecutor consider the media's role in reporting these cases? Does it matter whether or not the target of the investigation is a prominent person? Should a prosecutor use his or her discretion differently in terms of charging, plea bargaining, immunity, and potential punishment, depending on if the charges are for corruption or are for crimes of violence? How much should a prosecutor consider the quality and quantity of the evidence, the likelihood of a conviction, and the impact of a conviction on public safety and deterrence of future crimes? These are questions I and I'm sure many prosecutors think about.

Payoffs, Bribe Receiving, and Quid Pro Quos

Consider the following corruption cases:

1. Lobbyists for state casino operators seek to persuade state legislators to support a bill to legalize gambling. Casino operators, working through lobbyists, treat legislators to entertainment, offer lavish perks, and suggest that large political contributions will be made if they support the bill. Some of these lobbied lawmakers vote for the bill. Are they guilty of bribery?
2. A governor supports a referendum for a state lottery to raise money for school funding. An individual donates $500,000 to support the referendum. The governor thereafter appoints that individual to a state agency board. The governor receives nothing in return. Is he guilty of bribery?
3. A committee closely allied to a governor receives over $2 million from gambling interests. The committee uses the money for campaign-style

> television and radio ads supporting the governor's agenda. After the contributions are received, the governor includes a new initiative in his legislative agenda to expand gambling in the state. Is the governor guilty of bribery?

These cases are all based on real events. They involve the payment of money to influence the actions of government officials. To a prosecutor seeking to root out public corruption, these cases would appear to warrant criminal investigation. But the most critical element facing a prosecutor seeking to bring a charge of bribery against these officials and lobbyists would be to determine the following: Did lawmakers in case 1 vote to legalize gambling because of the perks and promised financial contributions? Did the governor in case 2 appoint the person to the state board because of his contribution to the lottery referendum? Did the governor in case 3 support legislation benefiting the gambling industry because of the $2 million donation to a political committee supporting his agenda?

To prove bribery, the payments must be made in return for an explicit promise or undertaking by the official to perform an official act. Thus, in each of the above cases, a prosecutor must prove—and a jury must find beyond a reasonable doubt—that there was a corrupt agreement, namely, that a benefit was given in exchange for something received. This element in legal parlance is called the "quid pro quo." It is a concept that is notoriously amorphous.

Cases 1 and 2 both come from Alabama and both cases were prosecuted before a jury. The jury in case 1, called the "State House Corruption Trial," acquitted everybody—state legislators, lobbyists, and industry moguls—of bribery and fraud. In case 2, however, the jury convicted the then-governor Don Siegelman of bribery. Case 3 involves the governor of New York State, Andrew Cuomo, who made public corruption and restoring public trust in government a centerpiece of his administration. With great fanfare, he created a state commission to investigate ethical misconduct by government officials.

It would seem that these cases all warrant criminal prosecution if the prosecutor has sufficient evidence of the quid pro quo. But proving a quid pro quo is extremely difficult. Such proof could come from the testimony of witnesses who personally participated in the corrupt scheme in either giving or receiving the payments. Proof could also come from recorded conversations by the participants containing statements admitting key facts relevant to the arrangement. Proof could also come from circumstantial evidence proving the agreement implicitly, such as proof of solicitations of benefits, the receipt and acceptance of benefits, and contemporaneous statements, writings, or official actions from which a corrupt exchange would be the only logical explanation.

However, the problem in all of these cases boils down to the reality of the contemporary political culture in which massive amounts of money are lavished by corporations and wealthy donors through their lobbyists for the specific purpose of influencing lawmakers—the messy, dirty, political "pay-to-play" culture of back-scratching, secret dealmaking, and unsavory favors. No matter how distasteful it is, the line between illegal bribery and lawful persuasion is often unclear, and given that uncertainty, there is the danger that innocent people might be dragged into the criminal net through arbitrary fact-finding and decision-making by ambitious prosecutors. Consider this question: If the line between lawful and unlawful conduct is so unclear, could not every president who appoints a campaign contributor as an ambassador, and every senator who puts forward a nominee for a federal judgeship after that person contributed to the Senator's campaign, be chargeable with bribery at the whim of a prosecutor, and convicted if a judge and jury go along?

Judges do make a difference in corruption trials. Indeed, the stark difference in verdicts in cases 1 and 2 may be attributable, in part, to the competence and ethics of the presiding judges. Alabama court observers have claimed that the judge in the Siegelman trial, Mark Fuller, harbored a strong bias against Siegelman. His bribery instruction to the jury has been assailed for diluting the quid pro quo requirement for a bribery conviction; he failed to advise the jury that it had to find an explicit promise or understanding. By contrast, the jury that acquitted the Alabama lawmakers and casino operators was correctly instructed by a respected federal district judge, Myron Thompson, who told the jury that it must find a "quid pro quo agreement," which he correctly defined as "a mutual understanding between the donor and the elected official that a campaign contribution is conditioned on the performance of a specific official action." The casino defendants contended that their conduct was inappropriate, maybe distasteful, but not criminal because there was no actual quid pro quo, and the jury agreed.

What about Governor Cuomo's conduct? The millions of dollars by the gambling industry to a committee supporting him, after which he pressed for new state legislation legalizing gambling, could be seen as a bribe depending on the evidence. There certainly is an appearance of impropriety. One of the commissioners on the governor's newly created Commission on Public Integrity was "stunned" by the disclosures. Once again, however, the need to prove a quid pro quo is what makes a corruption investigation so challenging. There may be innuendos and suggestions of corruption but that is not enough to convict. There must be proof of an actual quid pro quo. Allowing prosecutors such wide opportunities for charging bribery, as in the Siegelman case, may invite prosecutorial overreach. Indeed, the Siegelman case apparently was the first bribery prosecution predicated on an issue-advocacy campaign contribution.

Criminal statutes should not be so malleable that the boundary between lawful and unlawful conduct is too uncertain and unclear. As Sir Thomas More famously told the judges before they arbitrarily ordered his execution,

"The law is a causeway upon which, so long as he keeps to it, a citizen may walk safely." To be free of prosecutorial selectiveness, judicial abuse, and jury caprice, the causeway's edges need to be clearly marked, but with so many loopholes, hollows, and gaps, deciding to charge the crime of bribery may be a coin flip for some prosecutors, and that is not a result that inspires confidence in our criminal justice system.

The Supreme Court's McDonnell Case

Bob McDonnell, the governor of Virginia, was convicted in federal court of bribe-receiving for accepting lavish gifts from a political benefactor and, in return, bestowing broad access to government assistance and significant support for his commercial interests upon him. He appealed his conviction to the Supreme Court. The issue before the court was whether McDonnell, under the language of the bribery statute, "corruptly receive[d] a thing of value personally in return for being influenced in the performance of any official act." The proof at trial convincingly showed that McDonnell received valuable benefits from a donor named Jonnie Williams, head of a dietary supplement company, who bestowed these gifts on the governor and his wife and in return received the governor's help in promoting Williams's product, a supplement called Anatabloc.

Here are some examples of Williams's largesse: he gave McDonnell a $6,500 Rolex watch and use of his Ferrari on an expensive vacation; took the governor's wife to New York on a $20,000 shopping spree; gave the McDonnell's $120,000 in low-interest loans for their personal and business interests; took them on golf outings; and paid $15,000 in catering expenses for the McDonnell's daughter's wedding. McDonnell in return did the following: arranged meetings for Williams with state officials; permitted Williams to hold a luncheon at the governor's mansion to help him launch his new health product; and allowed Williams to draw up the guest list for another expensive reception at the governor's mansion to promote his product for health care leaders.

The jury that convicted McDonnell had ample proof that these exchanges were a quid pro quo, namely, that Williams's gifts to the governor were the "quid," and McDonnell's reciprocating his largesse the "quo." The jury apparently believed Williams's testimony that McDonnell always knew why Williams was showering the McDonnell family with gifts. Also critical was the close timing between Williams's gifts and loans to the governor and the efforts by McDonnell to help Williams and his company. This proof provided strong circumstantial evidence of prearrangement and coordination between Williams and McDonnell. Indeed, on one occasion, McDonnell directed a subordinate to meet with Williams on the same evening he returned from a free vacation at Williams's lake house. On another occasion, only six minutes after e-mailing Williams about a loan, McDonnell e-mailed an aide directing him to review studies at public universities that Williams wanted McDonnell's staff to conduct in connection with Williams's commercial products.

Notwithstanding the strong evidence of McDonnell's self-dealing and using the power of his office to benefit Williams, the Supreme Court reversed his conviction. The court ruled that McDonnell did not engage in any "official act" when he helped Williams. To criminalize what McDonnell did, according to the court, would convert routine political favors into corruption. Although their exchanges were "tawdry," according to the court, the arrangement did not involve the official exercise of government power. "Setting up a meeting, talking to another official, or organizing an event—without more—does not fit the definition of 'official act.'"

Construing the bribery law very narrowly, the court suggested that it was too vague and would allow prosecutors to overreach. To uphold the conviction, the court believed, would criminalize routine interactions between politicians and those who make political or personal donations to them. The court accepted McDonnell's argument that a government official who shows gratitude to a constituent, and provides access to officials who could help constituents with their problems, is not corruption. To criminalize such conduct, said the court, would make legitimate and commonplace favors for constituents unlawful.

The court gave a stern warning to prosecutors not to overreach when investigating corruption. The court admonished prosecutors that a public official's helping a donor gain a friendly ear, or inviting a constituent to a cocktail reception attended by persons in the donor's field of interest, were not the kinds of actions on which prosecutors should be allowed to base a prosecution because then prosecutors would have the power to indict any government official for any routine political favor. Of course, the court's admonishment begs the question; exactly what are those legitimate "routine political favors."

The court suggested that there is no workable standard to distinguish political favors from criminal acts, but of course that is not correct. To a prosecutor, political favors typically do not involve exchanges in which something is given by a donor to benefit a public official personally and in return for which the public official does something uniquely helpful for the donor. This is especially the case where, as in the McDonnell case, that exchange is animated by the public official's specific intention to enrich himself or herself and benefit the donor.

The court also appeared troubled by the statutory term "influence"; officials frequently are influenced by constituents to do favors for them. But again, if that favor for a constituent has been influenced by the constituent bestowing lavish gifts on the official specifically intended to buy that influence, it is difficult to see why that conduct should escape punishment. Surely the court was properly concerned that prosecutors should not use their huge powers to stretch the criminal law beyond what Congress intended. In fact, some prosecutors have brought dubious cases (see *U.S. v. Yates*) that the Supreme Court dismissed. But McDonnell was not a dubious case. The court's decision has made it much more difficult for prosecutors to root out corruption.

Colleagues Who Break the Law

I was working in the Homicide Bureau when I learned the stunning news. Gino Gibson, a former assistant district attorney in my office and thereafter a prominent defense lawyer, was gunned down execution-style in his Upper East Side apartment. According to the police and the medical examiner, Gibson was forced to kneel down as his killer shot him in the back of his head with a .25 caliber Beretta pistol. Gibson probably knew his executioner.

I knew Gino when he worked in the office. I was not very close with him, but I knew him well enough to know that I shouldn't be too shocked at the news. We talked from time to time; he had a wit dripping with sarcasm. He dressed well and had a smooth, sometimes overbearing manner. He had a reputation as an aggressive, ruthless prosecutor. He was a perfect fit for the Narcotics Bureau in which he worked for ten years during the height of New York's drug epidemic. Describing him as overzealous is too kind. You could hear him cursing at informants, cops, and staff from way down the hall. He was vilified by criminal defense attorneys but they were careful not to cross him. He was a gifted trial lawyer and jurors ate up his courtroom theatrics. He claimed never to have lost a trial, although a few of his convictions were thrown out by appellate courts for violations of trial rules.

I had no contact with Gino after he left the office but I followed his career. He always represented major drug traffickers. He was even more aggressive on the defense side, difficult as that is to believe. Judges and prosecutors loathed him, but he was tremendously effective and he definitely earned the huge fees he charged. He was investigated a few times, once for tax fraud and once for an ethics violation, but he always remained unscarred, until a bullet to the head killed him.

Nobody, except maybe a few of his clients, cried at Gino's funeral. I attended it out of curiosity, as well as a few other colleagues. Lots of lawyers and even a few judges showed up, including tons of media, and numerous undercover cops trying to blend in. Gino had no family to speak of so a clergyman who knew him tried to say some nice things.

For some reason, my bureau chief asked me to take on the Gibson case with two experienced homicide detectives to assist me. I really didn't want to do this but I agreed anyway. From the beginning, we assumed that the killing was likely drug-related. Gibson appeared to know his killer; there was no indication of a forced entry; nothing in the apartment was disturbed and nothing of value was taken. We did our best to assemble a picture of Gibson's professional work as a defense lawyer for the five years since he left the office. His law practice was solo. We obtained court records documenting every criminal case he handled, including his trials, guilty pleas, grand jury proceedings, and other records describing every client he had ever represented. Much of his work was in the state courts, but he also represented a few clients in the federal courts. For over a month, we examined thousands of pages of official court records and conducted dozens of interviews. Some persons talked to us, but many refused. We weren't ready to empanel a grand jury and compel witnesses to talk to us.

It was nearly a year into the investigation and we had come up empty so far. Then we got our first break. A defendant charged with possessing drugs—let's call him Tony—claimed he had information about the murder of a lawyer that my office might be interested in. He said, as informants invariably do, that he would be willing to trade his information in exchange for help in his case. We visited him in the jail's interview room. With his attorney at his side, Tony said that Gibson had represented him in a drug case a year before he was killed. Gibson told Tony that the large fee he was charging him was partly for "people in the D.A.'s office." He told us he did not get indicted; his drug case was dismissed after the assistant district attorney told the judge that the evidence against Tony had been discovered by police after an illegal search and that the case therefore could not be prosecuted successfully. Tony recalled that as they left court, he thanked Gibson who smiled and shook Tony's hand, but said nothing.

We immediately examined the court records in Tony's case. His description of the case and the court proceeding was accurate. The drug possession charge was dismissed. The docket entry contained notations of his lawyer's motion to dismiss and the prosecutor agreeing to the motion. The judge had written the words "Bad Search" on the court papers.

However, there was something peculiar about that case. The complaint described how the narcotics detectives, pursuant to a search warrant for drugs, entered an apartment, found a considerable stash of drugs, and arrested Tony, who was the only occupant in the apartment. The search warrant was attached to the case file. Contrary to what had been told to the judge in Tony's case, the warrant and the search itself appeared to have been perfectly proper. We found nothing in the records to indicate that there was anything irregular that would have supported a motion to dismiss the complaint based on unlawful police conduct.

We interviewed the narcotics detectives who had executed the warrant and asked them if they recalled the case. They did. Their stories were consistent. There was nothing unusual about the case. The warrant was easily supported by probable cause; they announced themselves and displayed the warrant prior to entering the apartment. They discovered a large quantity of drugs in different places and arrested Tony who was the only person in the apartment. We found nothing in the officers' actions that came even close to supporting a claim of illegality. So why did the assistant district attorney agree to drop the case?

We now turned our sights on the ADA, Donald Kaufman, who had asked the judge to dismiss the case. He was a senior assistant who had worked in the Narcotics Bureau for over fifteen years, many of those years alongside Gino Gibson. Kaufman had been offered the position as bureau chief but turned it down, claiming he preferred the give and take of courtroom litigation over administration. His bureau chief was not the most hands-on supervisor and actually looked to Kaufman for advice on cases. It appeared that Kaufman was able to select the cases he wanted and nobody ever questioned him about it. Kaufman always worked closely with the bureau's chief investigator, Manny Martinez, who had a reputation for using threats and occasionally violence to force defendants to become police informants. People referred to Kaufman and Martinez as a team. They worked together, ate lunch together, and went to ball games together. They were inseparable.

Sure enough, when we examined all of Kaufman's cases, we discovered that many of them involved Gino Gibson as the defense lawyer. There were a few actual trials between the two, and several guilty pleas, but there also appeared to be a disproportionate number of dismissals. We were stunned to find that virtually all of the dismissals appeared to be of questionable merit. They almost always were based on claims of unlawful police conduct, insufficiency of evidence, or an unwillingness to reveal the identities of informants.

Our examination of financial records confirmed our suspicions. There was a significant escalation in the financial portfolios of Kaufman and Martinez over the past five years. Both invested heavily in real estate and gambled frequently. We felt that we now had strong circumstantial evidence to connect them to a corrupt scheme to fix Gibson's drug cases, and maybe give us a clue to Gibson's murder.

Then came the real break. Alex Siegel, a law student and intern in the district attorney's office reported something very curious. Alex was having lunch with another intern at the coffee shop around the corner from the D.A.'s office. He and his friend were seated in a booth; in the booth behind them were two persons whom Alex recognized from the office. He heard mostly normal office talk and crime talk; someone was being investigated by the feds, he was going to make a deal, he was going to give them up to save himself. Siegel remembered hearing a reference to a "dead lawyer," or a "dead drug lawyer," or a "former assistant D.A." Siegel from photographs identified the two persons sitting in the booth behind him to be Kaufman and Martinez.

We knew that federal prosecutors had been investigating Gibson for bribery and tax fraud. The investigation ended when Gibson was killed. The feds, and everybody else, surmised that the killing was a retaliation by one of Gibson's disgruntled clients. Was it too far-fetched that Gibson's murder may have been engineered by an assistant district attorney and his chief investigator?

We interviewed Martinez first. We told him he wasn't being arrested yet but we gave him his Miranda rights anyway. Let's just say that after two or three hours of pretty intense interrogation, during which we explained that we had enough evidence to send him away from his friends and family for the rest of his life, he broke down and confessed. He said that he and Kaufman had been pocketing large amounts of cash from Gibson for several years for throwing cases. When Kaufman and Martinez learned that Gibson was being squeezed by the feds and might give them up, they decided to remove Gibson from the land of the living. Martinez, at Kaufman's suggestion, paid Frank Rivera, a former client of Gibson's, to do it.

Sadly, Rivera escaped official justice because he was murdered in a drug-related shooting. One might also argue that the ADA who helped engineer Gibson's murder also escaped official justice. After Kaufman learned that his buddy had given him up, he put the barrel of a gun inside his mouth and pulled the trigger. Only Martinez had to pay. He is presently sitting in a tiny cell in an upstate prison for the rest of his natural life.

Bugging a District Attorney's Office

In the aftermath of the Knapp Commission hearings in 1971, which unearthed rampant corruption by New York City police officials, prosecutors and police began to focus more extensively on misconduct by police and other government officials in the city's criminal justice system. Undercover operations had always been used, and deals had always been made with informants, spies, and stool pigeons to trap and catch corrupt officials. These operations became increasingly aimed at officials within the criminal justice system.

I was assigned at the time to the Rackets Bureau in the Manhattan D.A.s' office. I had investigated and prosecuted fraudulent practices in the city's municipal loan program, and had prosecuted several police officers accused of bribery, extortion, and other misconduct, so I was not surprised when one of the witnesses before the Knapp Commission contacted me about corruption in the Queens District Attorney's Office. Indeed, a recent federal search warrant had identified an assistant district attorney in the Queens office who was suspected of accepting bribes to fix cases. I was told about another individual—let's call him Sal—who was under investigation for insurance fraud and claimed that he was acquainted with a high-ranking executive in the Queens D.A.'s office, who he allegedly claimed had taken bribes to fix cases. I was also told that this Queens official had a close relationship with a criminal defense lawyer in New York County and that some of the cases that he fixed were in the criminal courts of New York County.

I related all of this to my bureau chief. I explained why I believed our office had jurisdiction to investigate another district attorney's office and what I thought were the risks going forward. Obviously this was a risky operation. He authorized me to go ahead with the investigation, keep him apprised, and be very careful.

The investigative team, which included at least eight other police officers from the Police Department's Internal Affairs Unit and officials from the city's inspector general's office, devised a plan to infiltrate the Queens D.A.'s office. The plan involved an acquaintance of Sal's, a man named Gerald Farber, who was a repeat narcotics offender who had been recently charged with another narcotics offense in Queens. Sal knew Farber. The plan was for Sal to approach the Queens official and ask for his help in the Farber case in return for money. Sal would record the conversation.

Getting Sal to my office from Queens for his instructions posed an unusual problem. Sal apparently suffered from some type of emotional illness that prevented him from traveling over bridges or underground on city subways, so in order to escort Sal to my office in Manhattan, the investigators, with Sal's consent, placed a pillow case over his head during the trip. Sal is very short, no more than five feet tall, and weighs over three hundred pounds. As he entered the building where my office was located, with a pillow case over his head and surrounded by at least eight large police officers, he must have made an indelible impression on the security guard at the desk.

We prepared Sal. The next morning, we recorded his call to his contact in the Queens D.A.'s office to set up a meeting for later that afternoon. Sal was equipped with a recording device that was monitored by our investigators. He entered the district attorney's office, met the official, and conversed for about twenty minutes. He told the official about the Farber case and asked him if he would be able to intercede for Farber with the people in the narcotics bureau. As Sal left the D.A.'s office and walked down the block to meet our investigators, he was suddenly accosted by detectives from the Queens D.A.'s office who immediately arrested him for offering a bribe to a member of the D.A.'s staff. Queens had itself recorded Sal trying to offer the bribe. Our investigators tried to intercede, explaining that Sal was an informant working for the Manhattan D.A's office. But we were in Queens, not Manhattan, and turf is power.

The media learned about this fiasco and had a field day, mostly at my expense.

Despite the best efforts of the Queens prosecutors, there was an insufficient basis to charge Sal with bribery; he lacked criminal intent, but the repercussions were toxic. The infiltration of another district attorney's office and the attempt to bribe a high-ranking official there created a serious rift between the two offices. The Manhattan District Attorney publicly apologized, and claimed that the operation was undertaken without sufficient cause. We never learned who tipped off our operation to Queens, but we suspected it was someone in the city's Department of Investigations.

Adding to my embarrassment, an appellate court reviewing a Queens conviction in a related case went out of its way to describe the attempt to infiltrate the Queens D.A.'s office and my role in the escapade. In describing the events, the court gratuitously referred to me by name, the kind of zinger that courts rarely do, especially with respect to prosecutors. I called the clerk of the court and asked him to request the court to remove my name from the published opinion. He told me to send a letter to the court giving my reasons. I did, and the court removed my name, referring to me merely as an assistant district attorney, but they made their point.

There is a final chapter to this bizarre story. I was summoned to appear before a federal grand jury. I was not told in advance the reason, but as I entered the witness room, and saw the clerk who was at the security desk when Sal was escorted into my office with a pillow case over his head and flanked by eight investigators, I immediately grasped the reason for my appearance. And when I went into the grand jury room and saw the scowling faces of the grand jurors, and was questioned about that night, I had the uncomfortable feeling that I was the target of an investigation into a violation of my informant's civil rights. After being thrown to the wolves by my boss, exposed by the media and the court as the architect of an investigative fiasco, and then subjected to a federal civil rights investigation, I wondered whether I had paid too steep a price for fighting corruption.

I remained in the district attorney's office for a few months, after which I left and joined the newly created special prosecutor's office, discussed above, tasked specifically with the mission to investigate and prosecute corruption.

Using Perjury to Fight Corruption

Perjury has always been seen as one of the most odious of crimes. Early treatises referred to perjury as "the most infamous and detestable of all crimes" and that "whoever gives false testimony must be thrown from the Tarpeian rock." Under the Code of Hammurabi, Roman law, and French law, death was the punishment for bearing false witness. In the colony of New York, punishment included branding the letter "P" on the offender's forehead.

However, the threat of charging a recalcitrant witness with perjury is critical to the successful investigation of corruption.

U.S. courts view perjured testimony as a flagrant affront to the fair and effective administration of justice. Prosecuting perjury is so important that prosecutors are allowed to use information even if it is acquired through illegal means. Many high-profile prosecutions have been for perjury: Lewis "Scooter" Libby, Vice President Dick Cheney's chief of staff, was convicted of lying to a federal grand jury about leaks of classified information to embarrass former CIA agent Valerie Plame; Martha Stewart was convicted of lying to federal investigators about a corrupt stock sale; Barry Bonds was convicted of giving false testimony over his use of performance-enhancing drugs; Mark Fuhrman pleaded no contest after being charged with perjury for denying during the O. J. Simpson trial that he ever used a racial epithet; and, of course, former president Bill Clinton was impeached for giving perjured testimony about his affair with Monica Lewinsky during his deposition in a sexual harassment lawsuit filed by Paula Jones.

Although false testimony can occur in virtually any legal proceeding, it often occurs during a prosecutor's investigation into substantive offenses such as official corruption, organized crime, financial fraud, and other crimes such as bribery, extortion, and obstruction of justice. Perjury in these investigations often is exposed during a grand jury's investigation into substantive crimes; it is unusual for a prosecutor to deliberately seek out perjury and then prosecute the witness for the perjury.

Proving perjury presents significant obstacles. A prosecutor needs to prove that the witness gave false answers under oath knowing that the answers were false and with the specific intention of deceiving the interrogator. Mistakes and memory lapses are common excuses. A witness's claim that he or she honestly believed what they were saying is hard to overcome. And ambiguous statements in the questions present an easy way for a witness to explain answers that appear to be false. An interrogator's questions must be unambiguous, clearly stated, and call for a clear response. For example, a prosecutor whose questions are vague or uses ambiguous language could not realistically expect to prove perjury. It is unlikely that a prosecutor could prove perjury against a witness who claimed a car was traveling "fast," or denied ever using "foul language," or denied "fixing" a case. These terms are too broad and subjective. It would be extremely difficult to prove that the witness knew that his answers were false, and intended to give an answer without actually believing that it was true.

However difficult it is, uncovering preexisting perjury is a legitimate task for a prosecutor but trying to trap someone into committing perjury in order to prosecute him is an entirely different matter. That type of conduct by prosecutors would seem highly irregular and illegitimate, and it is seen as a violation of principles of fairness embodied in the constitution's due process clause. Some prosecutors, however, during grand jury investigations into corruption might not consider it improper to deliberately manufacture a perjury charge in a grand jury where the actual corruption cannot be proven. Is trapping a witness into committing perjury a permissible prosecutorial technique?

Consider the following case. It's a real case with the names changed. Assume that a prosecutor is investigating corruption by judges and lawyers in the criminal justice system. Prosecutors have decided to investigate a judge named Alan Taub who was elected to the bench two years earlier after an eighteen-year career in private practice largely devoted to criminal defense. Based on reliable information, the prosecutor believes that Taub has current relationships with former clients involved in narcotics trafficking, especially Phillip Estella, also known as "Big Phil," reputedly the head of one of the city's largest narcotics operations who had been convicted of various federal and state racketeering and narcotics crimes.

Three police officers assigned to the investigation testified in the grand jury that they conducted extensive surveillance of Taub, during which they observed him in Estella's company several times. According to these witnesses, one month earlier, on May 15, the two men met in Times Square, spoke for about ten minutes, and then drove in Taub's car to Frank's Steakhouse in upper Manhattan where they remained for over an hour. After leaving the restaurant together and talking outside for several minutes, Estella was picked up by a black sedan, and Taub drove away in his car.

The prosecutor ostensibly summoned Taub into the grand jury to inquire about crimes of bribery and official misconduct. Taub was asked about his relationship with Estella. He said he had represented Estella as a lawyer in narcotics cases, but that after becoming a judge he had no contact with him. After a brief recess during which Taub conferred with his lawyer, he returned to the grand jury and corrected himself, now testifying that he remembered meeting Estella sometime in May outside Frank's steakhouse. The prosecutor then asked Taub the following questions:

Q. What were you doing there?
A. I was on my way into Frank's restaurant.
Q. What happened?
A. I saw Mr. Estella.

Q. What did you do?

A. We said hello, I asked him how he was. I knew he had just got out of prison. He said he was fine. He asked me how things were getting along. I said fine. That was it, as best as I remember.

Q. That was on the street?

A. That was on the street.

Q. What happened then?

A. I walked into Frank's and he walked into Frank's.

Q. What happened after you went into Frank's?

A. I had a drink.

Q, How long did that take?

A. About ten or fifteen minutes.

Q. What happened then?

A. I got up and left.

Q. Did you speak to Estella while you were having a drink?

A. Not that I recall.

Q. Did you have a previous arrangement to meet Estella at that location?

A. No, sir.

Q. It was purely by chance?

A. Yes.

Q. Can you remember anything else you and Estella talked about?

A. His health.

Q. Anything else?

A. No, it was just small talk.

Q. Did you discuss any matters that were in the courts?
A. No, sir.
Q. Did he discuss the fact that people in his organization were being arrested?
A. No, sir.

Based on his testimony, Taub was indicted for perjury. The specific counts in the indictment charged Taub with testifying falsely that he saw Estella for the first time in front of Frank's restaurant; that his meeting with Estella lasted about ten or fifteen minutes; and that he left the restaurant with Estella still inside the premises. Investigators on the surveillance team gave testimony contradicting Taub's answers.

But here is the critical question: Was the prosecutor using the grand jury in a legitimate manner to investigate corruption and individuals suspected of corruption or was the prosecutor using the grand jury to trap a witness into testifying falsely on minor outward details of a single meeting with a reputed criminal figure?

Several points need to be addressed. First, before concluding that the prosecutor's conduct is illegitimate, it must be shown that the prosecutor's purpose in summoning Taub into the grand jury and asking him about his relationship with Estella was to trap him into perjury. The meeting, although indiscreet, could easily have been a chance encounter with an individual whom the judge had previously represented while in private practice and was not material to the investigation. Moreover, there seems to be no showing that the prosecutor, by repetition, restatement, or elaboration ever pressed the witness into giving a convincing narrative of what actually happened inside the restaurant. Surely if the meeting was material to the investigation, the prosecutor would have made some discernible effort to demonstrate how this meeting was relevant to the grand jury's investigation and why false answers to peripheral details of the meeting would properly support a prosecution for perjury.

Further, the prosecutor made no effort to stimulate the witness's memory with information already acquired by the surveillance team to ascertain whether the witness was genuinely unable to recall details of an event that had no memorable significance. Because the intrinsic significance and memorability of the meeting appear to have been slight, should the prosecutor not have made a meaningful effort to refresh the witness's recollection? By failing to do so, did the prosecutor not demonstrate that his primary purpose was less to learn what happened than to trap the witness into committing perjury?

Most prosecutors can get witnesses to lie. Whether or not a prosecutor should be allowed to base a perjury indictment on the lies may depend on the significance of the lie, whether the lie materially obstructed the grand jury's investigation, and whether it appears from the interrogation of the witness that the prosecutor really wanted the truth, rather than the lie.

Justice Is Blind, but Is It Deaf?

Armed with a search warrant, Police Officers Steven Ross and Victor Diaz, partners assigned to New York City's Narcotics Task Force, forcibly entered the apartment of Ellen Adkins. They knew that her father, Frank Wilson, was a small-time drug dealer. Their plan was to threaten to jail Ellen on trumped up domestic abuse charges and take away her five-week-old daughter unless she called her father at his restaurant and made arrangements for him to come to the apartment immediately. Terrified, Ellen called her father and upon his arrival the officers demanded $6,000 from him, repeating their threats to harm his daughter if he did not comply. Wilson left and returned a short time later and gave the officers the money, whereupon they departed.

Two months later, Ross and Diaz visited Wilson's restaurant and told him his son was in trouble. They told Wilson it would cost him $12,000 to keep his son out of jail. This time Wilson reported the extortion attempt to the authorities. Wilson, according to a plan devised by the police department's Internal Affairs Unit, arranged to meet with Ross and Diaz in his restaurant. He was equipped with a recording device and $1,000 in marked money. The investigators were stationed in the basement. Ross entered the restaurant; Diaz stood guard outside. Wilson gave Ross $1,000 and explained that he would have the rest of the money the following day. As Wilson and Ross began to converse, it became apparent to the investigators that Wilson's recording device was not operating. One of the investigators opened a trap door in the back of the restaurant leading down to the basement, stood atop the ladder, and held a microphone over the edge to record the conversation. After Wilson paid Ross the money, the investigators arrested both officers. They were indicted for extortion, larceny, and conspiracy.

Prior to trial, the attorney for Diaz made a motion to sever the indictments so that each defendant would be tried separately. The court granted the motion. The prosecution elected to try Ross first. Before his trial, the judge held a hearing on the admissibility of the tape recording of the conversation between Wilson and Ross. Needless to say, given the unusual circumstances under which the conversation was recorded, the audibility of the recording was poor. Investigators brought in an acoustics expert to try to construct a reasonably accurate transcription of the recording, which under accepted trial rules would be given to the jury as an aid while they listened to the recording. The judge found that although significant portions of the tape were inaudible, there were enough clearly audible portions to make the recording admissible.

The prosecutor at Ross's trial presented the testimony of Wilson and his daughter, and the tape recording of the conversation in Wilson's restaurant. The defense called Ross. He did not deny discussing with Wilson the payment of money to him to prevent harm to his son and daughter, but Ross maintained that Wilson had propositioned him first, and that he was simply playing along in order to get evidence to arrest Wilson for bribery. On cross-examination, the prosecutor asked Ross the following questions relative to his claim that he was simply an honest cop trying to nail a corrupt drug dealer:

Question: Mr. Ross, prior to your meeting with Wilson, did you inform any of your supervisors that you had been propositioned by Wilson and intended to play along with his effort to bribe you?
Ross: No.
Question: In fact, Mr. Ross, from the day you were arrested until today in this courtroom, did you ever tell anybody that you were an honest cop trying to get evidence against a person who was trying to corrupt you?
Ross: No.

Ross was found guilty. Two weeks later his partner Diaz was scheduled to be tried, but things were very different now. First, the proof against Ross was very strong, but the proof against Diaz was weak. Diaz certainly was present when Ross tried to shake down Wilson, but he was outside the restaurant, and took no part in the conversation. Efforts to prove a corrupt connection between Ross and Diaz encountered further difficulties. Since Ross had already been convicted, the prosecution called him as its first witness. Ross refused to testify without immunity, but since immunity would be inconsequential unless his conviction were to be overturned, the prosecutor gave him immunity.

However, Ross gave virtually no relevant testimony. He claimed not to remember the event, and when the prosecutor tried to discredit his claim of lack of memory, the judge—a different judge than the judge in Ross's trial—refused to allow the prosecutor to attack his own witness. The only proof left to prove a corrupt conspiracy between Ross and Diaz was the tape recording.

Even though the recording had already been admitted at Ross's trial, the judge in Diaz's trial decided to make his own determination of whether or not to admit the tape. After playing the tape three times, with the aid of the transcript, the judge declared that he could hear nothing on the tape and refused to allow it into evidence. The prosecutor asked for a recess to consult his supervisors, after which the prosecutor made a motion for the judge to disqualify himself from the trial. The prosecutor argued that another judge had heard the tape and found it sufficiently audible to allow the jury to hear it. The prosecutor argued further that the judge should disqualify himself because he had difficulty hearing and wore a hearing aid. The judge responded, "I hear as well as anybody." The prosecutor replied:

> Your Honor, with all due respect, I disagree. And I respectfully request that Your Honor submit to a hearing test by a medical expert to test whether your hearing is so impaired that you should not preside at this trial.

As everyone in the courtroom undoubtedly heard, and as the transcript of the trial would memorialize for posterity, the judge then stated:

You dirty son of a bitch.

But the judge persisted in refusing to admit the tape. Without sufficient evidence to prove Diaz's guilt, the prosecutor dismissed the charges.

The judge was reported to the Judicial Conduct Commission and was sanctioned for his remark.

Chapter Nine

Prosecutors and Money

Profits or Justice?

How does money figure into the work of a prosecutor? Of course, cases involving thefts, bribes, extortions, and other financial frauds are the meat and potatoes in a wide range of criminal investigations and prosecutions, but that's not necessarily the sum of a prosecutor's work. There are many ways, apart from the prosecution of "money crimes," that money intrudes itself into the daily life of a prosecutor. Although most lawyers don't become prosecutors to get rich, there are instances when financial considerations may interfere with a prosecutor's role as a disinterested public servant with a commitment to justice.

For example, should special monetary incentives, rewards, and bonuses be used to enhance a prosecutor's performance? Is it ever appropriate for a prosecutor to make charging, plea bargaining, and dismissal decisions based on a defendant's willingness and ability to pay a fee to obtain favorable treatment? Money can become relevant in other ways. Would it be appropriate for a prosecutor to threaten a debtor or bad check writer with prosecution through a collection company? Is the prosecutor in such instances delegating her authority to a commercial entity to engage in quasi-prosecutorial functions? Finally, what about situations in which a prosecutor's office obtains large financial awards from the settlement of cases—maybe large settlements from the investigation of banks and corporations—or from confiscation and forfeiture of a defendant's property. Are there rules, standards, or guidelines to help determine how a prosecutor is allowed to spend the money and to whom a prosecutor should be accountable?

Cash for Convictions

To most prosecutors, serving as a prosecutor is an honor and a privilege. You serve your profession, your community, and the cause of justice. To these prosecutors, no special incentives or perks are needed to motivate them to work hard, perform at a high level, and behave ethically. Prosecutors certainly like to be recognized, and are not indifferent to seeing their names in headlines. In fact, there are prosecutors who keep scorecards of their courtroom victories and may even indulge in the self-inflating pronouncement: "I never lost a case." However, for most prosecutors, the incentives typically come from the gratification in protecting the community from lawbreakers, enforcing criminal laws responsibly and professionally, and serving the cause of justice fairly and impartially.

Some district attorneys, however, when evaluating the performance of their assistants, believe that sometimes it is appropriate to offer special rewards or bonuses for the performance of certain tasks. I recall that the district attorney under whom I worked offered higher salaries and bonuses to the assistants who were assigned to Part 30 of State Supreme Court—the "all-purpose" part—where felony cases were arraigned, evaluated by the assistants for purposes of disposition, and then resolved by guilty pleas, reductions of charges, and dismissals. To the district attorney, this was the most critical courtroom—the hub of the courtrooms designated for the felony trials—and it was staffed by the most experienced prosecutors. That these prosecutors were offered higher compensation seemed like an appropriate accommodation to their experience and the importance of their function.

Sometimes special rewards and bonuses need to be scrutinized more carefully to determine whether they really are an appropriate accommodation or simply a gratuitous payment that might create perverse incentives and unintended consequences. I learned about a district attorney who believed that she could improve the performance of her trial assistants through a special compensation program. She offered her assistants thousands of dollars in bonuses for hitting conviction targets that she established. The prosecutor, whose office handled felony prosecutions in several state counties, paid her assistants a bonus of $1,000 if they tried at least five felony cases in a year, with 70 percent of the trials ending in a felony conviction. Plea bargains or mistrials didn't count. Under her initiative several of her assistants netted an extra $5,000 a year.

The bonus is not an exorbitant amount. According to the district attorney, the bonus policy was established to encourage her prosecutors to meet minimum standards in line with trial and conviction statistics she claimed existed in other comparable jurisdictions. The money came from an office surplus, which she said is similar to incentive compensation plans used in private industry. "This is a trial office," the prosecutor declared. "If you are doing your job, you are going to necessarily go to trial." Although she acknowledged that it is difficult to articulate performance standards that accurately measure the work of trial attorneys, she contended that "this is the standard I think best meets the need to have a performance standard for trials that attorneys know and can be aware of and that does not in any way encourage any outcome in any specific case."

Although the standards do not overtly encourage prosecutors to seek any particular outcome in any specific case, the general linking of cash bonuses to convictions and making performance evaluations based on the goal of winning a conviction raise troubling questions. Indeed, it would seem that measuring a prosecutor's performance by winning a case is a dubious test under any circumstances. There are outstanding prosecutors who skillfully try very difficult cases and lose. Under this district attorney's plan, even though these prosecutors performed at the highest level, they would not qualify for a bonus.

Also, there is the ever-present danger that a prosecutor seeking a bonus might alter his or her behavior to obtain the bonus. For example, a prosecutor in preparing a case for trial might evaluate the case based on the chances of losing it and losing the bonus, rather than on whether or not justice would be served by proceeding to trial. Assuming the prosecutor was convinced of the defendant's guilt of a serious crime but worried about his or her ability to present a strong enough case to the jury, would a prosecutor focused on getting a bonus decide not expend his energy on what may be a losing case? In fact, a prosecutor focused on a bonus might be more likely to seek a plea disposition even though the deal might not be in the public's best interest. Might that prosecutor concentrate his or her efforts on taking a case to trial that would more likely result in a conviction? Conversely, a prosecutor interested in getting a bonus might be less inclined to take a plea in a case that looks like a sure winner at trial, even though a plea disposition might be in the public's best interest.

Even more worrisome is the possibility that financial incentives might encourage some prosecutors to alter their courtroom conduct to improve their chances of getting a conviction. It is indisputable that some prosecutors bent on winning convictions at all costs might more be predisposed to break the rules. This phenomenon is easily documented in convictions that have been reversed based on a prosecutor's violation of discovery rules, presenting inadmissible evidence, or making inflammatory arguments to the jury. Would a cash bonus for getting a conviction be an additional incentive to cause the prosecutor to deviate from the rules to win?

Many prosecutors probably would echo the sentiment of former Denver district attorney Mitch Morrissey that hard work doesn't always pay off in the jury box, and that prosecutors should not be motivated by monetary incentives and conviction rates. According to Morrissey, "I would worry that if something is tied to a conviction rate, an assistant wouldn't try a hard case that required a trial. We want people trying cases that need to be tried. If they don't win, they don't win."

Stan Garnett, the district attorney of Boulder County, Colorado, does not discount the importance of taking cases to trial, but notes that prosecutors engage in many other tasks that can measure performance. He looks at how his prosecutors comport themselves ethically, manage their dockets effectively, and relate with local law enforcement, as well as whether they take cases to trial or plead out too many cases. "I want my assistants on trial as much as possible," Garnett says, "but I want them focused on doing the right thing on their cases. I don't want them distracted by some kind of bonus or award."

Prosecution is certainly an adversarial profession and every prosecutor wants to win his or her trials. Nor is there any dispute that winning a conviction is an appropriate prosecutorial objective, legally and ethically, and is one way to properly measure a prosecutor's performance. But equally important, of course, is the constitutional and ethical mandate on prosecutors to serve justice as well. To the extent that a prosecutor's compensation is based on the number of cases he or she takes to trial, and the number of convictions he or she obtains, the prosecutor's judgment and discretion may be affected, and other reasonable options and dispositions may be discounted or overlooked.

One might justify this program as a reasonable way to encourage trial prosecutors to perform at a high level. Clearly, if you are doing your job properly, you are necessarily going to go to trial some of the time. The district attorney claimed to have set the standard low enough so that her prosecutors would not be selecting the easiest cases from their 150 to 175 cases a year, and high enough so that prosecutors could demonstrate they have certain trial skills and good judgment. It is also worth noting that prosecutors assigned to more complicated or lengthy cases would be exempt from the requirement.

Needless to say, this approach engendered controversy. Defense lawyers moved to dismiss cases based on the bonus plan. Other critics complained that there are better ways of spending limited financial resources, especially in a time of shrinking law enforcement budgets. In the end, the duality of a prosecutor's role—an aggressive advocate and a champion of justice—may be incompatible with cash incentives. Can a prosecutor really seek justice when winning a case is tied to making money?

Money for Mercy

Prosecutors, when making choices about what cases to prosecute, may decide to show leniency instead of aggressively prosecuting them. One initiative used by prosecutors allows a defendant to avoid trial, punishment, and a criminal record. It is called diversion. Prosecutors use diversion to reduce heavy caseloads, to focus the prosecutor's attention on more serious crimes, and to give minor offenders a chance to get on with their lives without the burden of a criminal record. Diversion fits within a prosecutor's broad discretion to enforce the criminal law. Diversion typically is offered to first-time offenders, minor narcotics offenders, and other low-risk offenders. Diversion is supposed to be a salutary alternative to criminal punishment. It is an effort to moderate the harsh penalties of the criminal law so as not to stigmatize persons with a criminal record and help rehabilitate them. Diversion is often conditioned on the offender undergoing treatment alternatives or other programs that best serve the ends of justice.

According to the standards of the National District Attorney's Association, diversion should be used responsibly in the interest of justice, both to the community and to the individual. Relevant factors include the nature of the offense, any special characteristics of the offender, whether the defendant is a first-time offender, the likelihood that the defendant will benefit from the program, the extent to which diversion will enable a defendant to maintain employment or remain in school, the likelihood that the defendant will recidivate, and the need to treat similarly situated defendants equally.

Most prosecutors use diversion responsibly, but some don't. Some prosecutors abuse the program by actually demanding money from vulnerable offenders in lieu of prison and a criminal record. Diversion also allows prosecutors the opportunity to show favoritism to friends. One of the most notorious examples of a prosecutor abusing diversion to fill the law enforcement coffers and reward friends is Douglas Valeska, long-time district attorney of Henry County, Alabama. His record as a prosecutor is replete with cases of wrongful convictions, planting evidence, retaliation, and unfair prosecutions. Several of his convictions were vacated by appellate courts because of racial discrimination in the selection of juries. Many of his death penalty convictions were reversed because of misconduct. Valeska's appalling persecution of Lee Carroll Brooker, a seventy-seven-year-old disabled veteran, for growing marijuana in his backyard and sending him to prison for life without parole has been noted in Chapter 1.

Valeska's misuse of diversion has also attracted considerable attention. During his three decades as district attorney, Valeska operated what one commentator called a "dismissal for sale scheme, available only to those with money and, in some cases, favor." Given the fact that the county is poor, rural, and includes a very large black population, it should not be surprising that poor and minority offenders would be at a distinct disadvantage in terms of being granted diversion. Indeed, the fees extracted by Valeska under his diversion program are among the highest in the country. The fees have generated more than $1 million for Valeska's office in the past five years, but it is often the case that minority and poor offenders are denied the opportunity for diversion because of lack of funds. Valeska's policy was not to waive or reduce fees for poor defendants, many of whom would likely qualify for diversion but were unable to pay.

For Valeska, if an offender is willing and able to pay, money can buy a limitless number of second chances. Take, for instance, the case of Jared Manuel. He was granted diversion three times for property crimes, then pleaded guilty to transmitting obscene materials to a child, then was granted diversion again by Valeska to seven new drug charges, after which he was arrested again on sex offender registration requirements. Valeska collected over $10,000 from Manuel in diversion fees that allowed Manuel to avoid prison.

Manuel's fees were consistent with fees Valeska typically charged—$750 for a misdemeanor and $1,400 for a felony. The money had to be paid up front and Valeska assessed a fee for each criminal charge. So, in a prescription drug fraud case where the defendant faced seven separate counts, he had to pay almost $10,000 for diversion. Valeska's office retained the bulk of the money and spent it any way it wanted. Although it is not clear whether or not race was a variable in Valeska's diversion decisions, there is no question that money was the deciding factor.

Favoritism may also have been at play when Valeska granted diversion. Consider the case of Harvey Burch, twenty-eight years old, who got drunk at a party and fired a gun over the crowd and then started spraying Mace. He fled the party in the backseat of a car driven by a friend and was arrested after the car was stopped by a deputy sheriff. The car was driven by Douglas Valeska II, Valeska's son. Valeska went to the scene and took his son home. Burch was found in possession of a gun, a loaded magazine, a knife, pepper spray, and drugs. He was charged with gun and drug possession, but not with firing a weapon or spraying Mace. Burch was not prosecuted. Valeska granted him diversion on the condition he pay $2,500 in diversion fees. His case was later dismissed. The diversion money, according to the arresting officer, was used to buy scuba gear for the Sheriff Department's dive team. The arresting officer was the captain of the dive team.

Although Valeska refused to reveal how he spent the diversion money, documents from former employees revealed that the money was allocated to purchase equipment for police such as guns, rifles, and holsters; for conferences, training, and travel; for retirement parties; and for courtroom attire for his staff. After a cashier at a local restaurant was charged with using a customer's debit card to buy $14 worth of food, Valeska demanded she pay $2,000 for diversion. Valeska used the payment for his office's expenses, and for two charities he founded and on whose boards he served. A comparison with other wealthier counties shows that diversion fees typically are capped at well under $1,000.

Contrast Valeska's indulgence in the Harvey Burch case with the way he treated Jarvis Bracy, twenty-five years old, black, with a wife and young child, who earned $200 a week working part time at a restaurant. Bracy was charged with a felony on his first offense—misidentifying himself to a police officer while he was drunk one night. Bracy was riding in a friend's car when they were stopped by the police. Suspecting he was on drugs, the officers asked Bracy for his name and ran a warrant check. Bracy spelled his last name with an E, B-R-A-C-E-Y, and gave a social security number with two incorrect digits. The misstatements would have been a misdemeanor but Bracy had several unpaid traffic tickets, so giving false information to evade arrest became a felony.

Since he had no prior record, Bracy was offered pretrial diversion but at an amount he could not pay: $3,730. He was able to pay only $215. Valeska refused diversion but retained the money, presumably to cover the unpaid parking tickets. Bracy, with a new family and seeking to keep a clean record, kept asking for diversion. He even completed a substance abuse class and fifty hours of community service. However, despite working two other jobs, he could only come up with $900 more, which was not enough. Bracy offered to pay in $50 monthly installments, but Valeska refused, and kept the $900.

When Bracy's diversion was rejected, he asked for a trial. Assisted by a clearly inadequate defense lawyer—not uncommon in Henry county—Bracy was found guilty after a fifteen-minute trial and became a felon. The burdens of raising a family and seeking better employment are weightier with a criminal record, but Bracy persevered. "You try your best to smile every day," he said.

Valeska's authoritarian rule is over. An investigation by the Alabama Ethics Commission found that Valeska forced members of his staff to campaign for him and donate money, spent lavishly on travel, and used his employees to perform personal chores like cutting down trees on his property. He was found guilty and fined. He did not seek reelection. The new prosecutor, who previously worked to rehabilitate prisoners, is said to have a more merciful approach to prosecution, and diversion, than Valeska.

Prosecutors as Debt Collectors

One of the most perverse ways that some prosecutor offices make money is to contract with debt-collection companies and allow the companies, for a fee, to use the official letterhead and stationary of the prosecutor's office to send threatening letters to persons owing money and persons alleged to have written bad checks advising them they will be jailed unless they pay up on their debts. This practice, although clearly unethical, is widespread throughout the United States. Hundreds of prosecutors allow their offices to be used this way because it makes money for them.

The nation's two biggest collection companies, CorrectiveSolutions and BounceBack, have for many years contracted with prosecutor offices to collect bad debts by falsely informing the debtor that the collection letter is being sent by the prosecutor and that failure to pay will result in prosecution. By contracting with these companies and allowing them to use their stationary, prosecutors are complicit in this fraudulent practice. In the first half of 2012, CorrectiveSolutions sent out 17,000 letters on behalf of the Los Angeles District Attorney's Office.

Debt collection is a hugely profitable business, netting the companies millions of dollars in fees, which they share with the prosecutors. The tactic of bullying and threatening criminal prosecution under the guise of the district attorney's seal is clearly fraudulent, not only because the prosecutors are not involved in writing or sending out the letters, but also because no crime may even be involved. Owing money is not a crime and writing a bad check is not a crime unless it is committed with an intent to commit fraud.

Numerous lawsuits have been brought against collection companies but the tactic continues. The lawsuits have alleged a violation of the Fair Debt Collection Practices Act based on the companies' impersonating the district attorney's office and making false and misleading threats to prosecute and jail anyone who does not make good on the debt. Numerous judgments have been awarded against collection companies but this has not dampened the companies' use of this tactic. Ironically, some prosecutor's offices have even filed friend of the court briefs—known as amicus curiae briefs—which typically are filed by groups having a strong interest in the litigation, in this case in support of the collection companies.

Prosecutors strongly defend this practice. A spokesperson for the district attorney of Suffolk County, Massachusetts, stated: "It's hugely beneficial to taxpayers because we as prosecutors can then assign resources to more violent crimes and save taxpayers thousands of dollars every year." The spokesperson for the district attorney of Middlesex County, Massachusetts, said, "Those who have committed a crime of larceny are given the opportunity to avoid criminal prosecution while the victim merchants have the opportunity to have the matter addressed in lieu of filing a criminal complaint."

Sometimes a prosecutor's involvement in debt collection may be lawful. For example, the U.S. Supreme Court unanimously upheld a private debt collector's use of a prosecutor's letterhead to make people pay when such conduct is allowed under the state's law. In that case, *Sheriff v. Gillie*, an Ohio law authorized the state attorney general to appoint a private special counsel to collect debts owed to the state and to use the attorney general's letterhead for that purpose. According to the Supreme Court, since the special counsel is acting on the state's behalf, and seeking payments owed to the state, there is no false or misleading conduct by the debt collectors.

By contrast, the American Bar Association's Standing Committee on Legal Ethics recently wrote a formal ethics opinion condemning as unethical the actions of prosecutor's offices in allowing debt collectors to use their official letterheads to collect debts. The ethics opinion found that by providing debt collection companies with the prosecutor's official letterhead to be used in the demand letters, the prosecutors violated Model Rule 8.4 that states that "it is professional misconduct for a lawyer to engage in conduct involving dishonesty, fraud, deceit or misrepresentation." The letter clearly creates the false impression in the mind of the consumer that the letter was coming directly from the prosecutor's office and threatens prosecution and jail unless the debtor pays up.

According to the ethics opinion, the problem is that the letters purport to come from a prosecutor's office "when no lawyer from the prosecutor's office reviews the case file to determine whether a crime has been committed and prosecution is warranted or reviews the letter to ensure it complies with the rules of professional conduct." The opinion notes that prosecutor's offices have felt the financial pinch of government budget cutbacks, and that "occasionally practices have taken hold in prosecutor's offices that, while driven by budgetary exigencies, fall short of their higher calling."

Aside from engaging in fraudulent and deceitful conduct in violation of ethics rules, a prosecutor who provides its official letterhead to debt collection companies without conducting any review of the letter drafted by the company or making any determination whether a crime has been committed by the debtor also violates another ethics rule, Model Rule 5.5, by assisting the debt-collection companies in engaging in the unauthorized practice of law. In the collection area, a nonlawyer cannot give legal advice, institute litigation, or threaten to sue on behalf of another.

As of now, Oregon is the only state that prohibits prosecutors from allowing debt collection companies to use their letterheads. Whether or not Oregon's law will set a trend remains to be seen.

Prosecuting for Profit

One of the most viable ways for prosecutors to enrich themselves and their offices is to go after the property of persons they prosecute—their cars, yachts, planes, bank accounts, and any other assets they possess. The process of asset forfeiture and confiscation has been used by law enforcement for decades. It is a familiar tool to combat crime but also controversial because this power can be easily abused.

Asset forfeiture laws allow law enforcement officials to seize a person's property when there is reason to believe that the property was connected to criminal activity, or is the proceeds of criminal activity. The person from whom the property is seized need not be charged with or even suspected of any criminal behavior. It is the property itself that is alleged to be connected to the crime. Under very broad regulations, and with little procedural protections or judicial oversight, a person can be ordered to disgorge to the prosecutor all of his or her property that is suspected of being tainted by his unlawful conduct. Needless to say, the assets can be a hugely profitable cash cow to a prosecutor's office, especially at a time when budgets are shrinking.

Without significant accountability and transparency, asset forfeiture laws can be misused. Prosecutors might more readily select cases for prosecution that could yield significant financial benefits, even if there is little basis to bring or maintain criminal charges. For example, there are many cases in which large amounts of money are discovered in cars and homes. In some jurisdictions, carrying a large amount of cash, while not in and of itself unlawful, may provide sufficient grounds to suspect the commission of a crime. The burden is typically on the individual who owns the seized cash to prove his or her innocence and that the cash is unconnected to criminal activity. Otherwise, prosecutors can keep the money.

Under the law, forfeited assets must be used for law enforcement–related purposes such as narcotics enforcement, drug treatment, and crime-prevention programs, but there are many cases in which prosecutors have used forfeited assets for purely personal reasons unconnected to any legitimate law enforcement purpose. One prosecutor used a portion of forfeited assets to live rent free for five years in a house that a judge had ordered seized and sold at auction. Another prosecutor used $5,000 from a forfeiture fund to pay off his student loan debt. Forfeiture money has been used for district attorneys' retirement parties and office equipment.

Conversely, there are cases in which prosecutors have used legitimately obtained assets for benevolent reasons, particularly in criminal cases in which a defendant facing prosecution agrees to pay financial penalties to avoid going to trial and getting found guilty. This often happens in the prosecution of large financial institutions accused of financial fraud who agree to a so-called "deferred prosecution agreement" in lieu of a trial. In a recent settlement under this arrangement, three major banks—BNP Paribas, HSBC, and Standard Chartered—were accused by the Office of New York County district attorney Cyrus Vance of violating United States sanctions by secretly transferring billions of dollars to Iran, Cuba, and Sudan. To avoid a trial, the banks agreed to pay over $10 billion dollars in penalties. Vance's office secured a windfall of $808 million from the penalties, nearly ten times his office's annual budget. How he used that money has received considerable attention, and scrutiny.

Vance decided to use the almost once-in-a-lifetime bonanza to support new programs and technologies throughout the country that could have a lasting impact on crime control and prevention. According to Vance, given the windfall, "there is a window of opportunity here to make transformative investments" in crime control and crime prevention. Consider one of his prominently reported grants—an award of $38 million in grants to thirty-two jurisdictions in twenty states across the United States to eliminate backlogs of untested "rape kits." These kits contain DNA evidence that could identify perpetrators, prevent future offenses, and even exonerate innocent persons. Under Vance's awards, which range in amount from $97,000 to $2 million, an estimated 56,475 rape kits will be able to be tested. Interested jurisdictions were invited to submit applications providing information about the size and scope of their backlogs, their current testing policies, and their willingness to follow best practices determined by the New York District Attorney's Office and its partners.

Another of Vance's high-profile grants was $101 million to be allocated to fund new initiatives to enhance security at New York City Housing Authority developments. The money would pay for new infrastructure upgrades such as additional interior and exterior security cameras, exterior permanent lighting, new doors, and keyfob access. According to Vance, this funding not only enhances residential safety but also demonstrates "a commitment to fairness in the criminal justice system and the belief that a crime prevented is better than a crime prosecuted."

Vance's grants make him an unusual Santa Claus to the law enforcement community, with a bundle of goodies being handed out to subsidize the kinds of reform efforts that too often elude implementation for lack of funds. Vance has invited applications from many interested quarters. For example, he was sold on the application by John Jay College of Criminal Justice in New York to create a new institute akin to the Harvard Kennedy School to educate the nation's prosecutors and study how they can rectify shortcomings in the criminal justice system. Vance earmarked over $250 million for crime prevention, including $90 million to the New York City Police Department to provide thousands of smartphones and tablets for officers. Vance is funding cybercrime labs in prosecutors' offices, providing new training and equipment at the city's medical examiner's office, and giving millions to state agencies for expenses like license plate readers and a photographic database of convicted felons. In a potentially ground-breaking initiative, Vance has allocated $25 million to start a nonprofit clearinghouse for gathering data about cyberattacks—called the Global Cyber Alliance—which will enable his staff to disseminate information quickly about attacks in financial capitals around the world. The initiative comes from Vance's belief that computer-based crime is the greatest threat to New York City outside of terrorism.

The ability of Vance, or any prosecutor, to be able to spend substantial sums of money without any real oversight raises questions about how the money is being spent, and whether there is sufficient transparency. Vance is authorized by law to spend the money as he sees fit. Critics have complained that the revenue should more properly go to the city. They contend that the grants should be subject to auditing, and that there should be formal policies in place for distributing the money. Vance has allowed the comptroller to inspect his books, but as he has observed: "There's always going to be people who disagree with my choices."

In an unprecedented and extraordinary way, Vance has placed himself at the center of the debate on how to rebuild a broken criminal justice system. His unique approach will be closely watched.

Chapter Ten

The Prosecutor as a Minister of Justice

Fair Blows and Foul Blows

The public image of the prosecutor, whether elected or appointed, often depends on sensational trials and investigations that he has led. Prosecutors have been romanticized and vilified. It's hard not to root for a "rackets-busting" special prosecutor like Thomas E. Dewey who prosecuted gangsters Dutch Schultz and Lucky Luciano; or Los Angeles prosecutor Vincent Bugliosi who prosecuted Charles Manson and his cult for the grisly "Helter-Skelter" murders of actress Sharon Tate and Leno and Rosemary LaBianca; or Preet Bharara, the federal prosecutor who single-handedly convicted a record number of lawmakers in New York State government. On the other hand, some prosecutors, like New Orleans district attorney James Garrison, to advance his own career, relentlessly pursued a fraudulent prosecution of businessman Clay Shaw for conspiring with Lee Harvey Oswald to assassinate President John F. Kennedy;

or Texas prosecutor Ken Anderson, who deliberately suppressed evidence of Michael Morton's innocence that resulted in Morton's conviction and imprisonment for twenty-five years.

How should the public view the role of the prosecutor? Probably the most famous description about the prosecutor's role was in the 1935 Supreme Court decision *Berger v. United States*. The *Berger* case has attained near-iconic status for its portrayal of the prosecutor's duty to serve justice, play by the rules, and not hit below the belt.

> The prosecutor is the representative not of an ordinary party to a controversy, but of a sovereignty whose obligation to govern impartially is as compelling as its obligation to govern at all, and whose interest, therefore, in a criminal prosecution is not that it shall win a case, but that justice shall be done. As such, he is in a peculiar and very definite sense the servant of the law, the twofold aim of which is that guilt shall not escape or innocence suffer. He may prosecute with earnestness and vigor—indeed he should do so. But while he may strike hard blows, he is not at liberty to strike foul ones. It is as much his duty to refrain from improper methods calculated to produce a wrongful conviction as it is to use every legitimate means to bring about a just one.

Berger's powerful rhetoric about prosecutors striking "fair blows," not "foul blows," continues to resonate with courts, prosecutors, and commentators. Indeed, there is something heroic about a prosecutor who is required to play by special rules that may require him to eschew winning a case for the higher principle of serving the cause of justice. Can prosecutors really do that?

Confessing Error

Prosecutors make mistakes. Sometimes the mistakes are excusable; they misunderstand the applicable rules, miscalculate the strength of the evidence, or overlook critical facts or law that might change their approach to a case. Sometimes the mistakes may involve a reckless indifference or disregard for the proper exercise of prosecutorial power. However, if a responsible prosecutor recognizes a mistake, the prosecutor should try to correct it, even if that involves making a "confession of error" to a court.

I recall one such case. I was in the Appeals Bureau when a case was assigned to me. According to the record, a police officer named Beedenbender (how can one forget that name) was directing traffic in mid-Manhattan on a sunny spring afternoon when he observed a motorist driving an automobile bearing Virginia license plates. Beedenbender recognized the driver; he had previously arrested him for possessing drugs and believed there was an outstanding warrant or "hold" on him. Beedenbender followed the motorist in his patrol car to the next red light where he emerged from his car, approached the defendant, and directed him to pull around the corner and park in front of the precinct station house. Beedenbender then directed him to come with him into the precinct. After learning that the warrant was still outstanding, Beedenbender placed the defendant under arrest, advised him of his rights, and started the booking process on the second floor. During the booking process, Beedenbender went downstairs and back to the car, which was parked in front of the stationhouse and searched it. He found a .45 caliber revolver under the driver's seat. About ten minutes had elapsed from the time the defendant had been brought into the precinct until Beedenbender searched the car. No warrant authorized the search. The defendant was charged with possessing the gun, a class D felony.

After his arraignment, the defendant made a motion to suppress the gun based on his claim that the gun was discovered during an unlawful search of his car and therefore, under the Fourth Amendment's exclusionary rule, it was required to be suppressed and not used as evidence. A judge denied the motion, finding that the search was lawful and the gun lawfully discovered. The defendant then pleaded guilty but preserved his right to appeal.

When I received the appeal, I began to research the rules under the Fourth Amendment governing warrantless searches of automobiles. Today, there is a considerable body of constitutional law dealing with searches of automobiles. In fact, there is even a special category of police searches entitled "Automobile Searches" which is a well-recognized exception to the constitutional requirement that police officers must first obtain a search warrant before conducting a search into someone's private space.

However, at the time of my research, the law of warrantless searches generally was quite limited, but I did locate a precedent that seemed to apply. The U.S. Supreme Court had held that warrantless police searches could be undertaken when the search was "incident to an arrest," meaning that the search of the person arrested and his or her belongings had to be roughly contemporaneous with the arrest.

In conducting my research I worked under the supervision of a bureau chief who was unequivocally the finest and most brilliant lawyer I have ever known—Michael Juviler. Together we read and reread leading cases, including *Preston v. U.S.*, which squarely held that searches incident to an arrest could not be conducted without a warrant if the search occurred at a different place than the arrest, and at a time well after the arrest had been made. I found no decisions that contradicted or diminished the *Preston* rule.

We brainstormed through many long days and evenings trying to come up with some plausible legal argument to justify the search. After much legal soul-searching, we concluded that there was no legal justification for the search. But the case obviously presented an awkward situation for our office. We believed our office had made a mistake in litigating the case at the suppression hearing and we felt we needed to correct our office's mistake and acknowledge that the search was unlawful and the defendant's conviction needed to be vacated.

We met with district attorney Frank Hogan. We informed him of our position about the constitutional infirmity of the conviction. We told him we could not in good faith make a responsible appellate argument to justify the legality of the search and therefore felt we had a duty to advise the appellate court of our position. The district attorney listened carefully. It didn't take him long to respond. He told us to do what we thought was the right thing to do even if that meant confessing his office's mistake.

After the defendant filed his brief in the Appellate Division seeking to have his conviction vacated because of the unconstitutional search, we responded in our own appellate brief in which we agreed with the defendant's position; in effect we "confessed error." Our brief set out the facts objectively, analyzed the applicable precedents, and gave our conclusion: the search of the defendant's car was unlawful under the applicable law, the discovery of the gun was the fruit of the unlawful search, and without evidence of the gun, the criminal charge of gun possession should have been dismissed.

The legal journey was just beginning. I arrived at the Appellate Division on the day assigned for the argument of the appeal feeling a bit uneasy. I expected to make my argument after the defendant's lawyer made his, but to my surprise, the defendant's attorney did not show up to argue the appeal. Why should he, I thought? The district attorney was representing his client as effectively as he could have done.

When the case was called, I stood up and began to argue why my office believed the conviction should be vacated. The panel seemed unpersuaded. Several of their questions showed that the judges were uncomfortable, maybe even annoyed, with my position. "Wasn't there a sufficient unity of time and place to justify the search as an incident to the arrest?" asked one of the judges. It was an embarrassing ordeal to make an argument that appeared to run counter to the prosecutor's mission to vindicate the rule of law and punish lawbreakers. I believed my office was following the ethical ideal that a prosecutor is supposed to embrace, namely, to serve the cause of justice over the goal of winning.

There was one judge, however, who appeared to align himself with my office's position. He had a reputation as a careful, responsible, and fair-minded judge. He asked questions that appeared to support my position as I struggled through my argument. "The defendant was in custody and his car immobilized," he said. "Didn't the officer have time to go to a judge and get a warrant to search the car?" "Wasn't he simply fishing for evidence?" It seemed clear to him that the police officer had overreached.

Two months later, the panel affirmed the lower court's ruling that the search was lawful and rejected our confession of error, but my ally on the bench wrote a strong dissent that mostly tracked the argument in our brief. He also gave permission to the defendant to appeal the case to the state's highest court, the Court of Appeals. Just imagine this picture: The district attorney is now poised to ask the state's highest court to overturn a decision in which the intermediate appellate court affirmed the defendant's conviction.

Not surprisingly, the media found the story unusual and provocative. I seem to recall a headline "D.A. Fights for Conviction and Then Throws in the Towel." I admit that I continued to go over and over in my mind the facts of the case and struggled to avoid second-guessing our decision to "throw in the towel."

Once again, we wrote a strong appellate brief in the Court of Appeals, and once again the defendant's lawyer did not show up to argue the case. I always enjoyed traveling up to Albany to the majestic courthouse on Eagle Street where lawyers argue important appeals in the elegant wood-paneled courtroom with the portraits of all the former judges staring down at them. Some of the judges' law clerks passed me by in the hushed corridors near the library. They knew me from previous arguments, although on this occasion I felt they looked at me as if I had some kind of disease. Once again, I was roughed by some of the judges, but this time around most of the judges seemed much more skeptical of the lawfulness of the search.

The result this time was different. The court unanimously reversed the conviction and dismissed the indictment. Its brief opinion endorsed my office's position.

So we won, or lost, depending on one's view of a prosecutor's ethical role in serving justice. Justice is indeed a difficult concept. It involves judgments about values. The defendant was guilty of possessing a gun unlawfully, but the government was guilty of violating his constitutional rights. Ultimately it is the responsibility of the prosecutor to choose which value to champion.

Is the Defendant Innocent?

Years ago, when I became a prosecutor, I was trained to believe that you never put a defendant to trial unless you were personally convinced of his guilt. This was the accepted ethos in my office and, I assumed, of prosecutors' offices generally. I never questioned that precept. But how does a prosecutor attain that level of confidence? What kind or degree of proof establishes confidence in a finding of guilt? Proof is so varied, quantitatively and qualitatively. Prosecutors may try to behave fairly but the proof is often ambiguous; there is never certainty.

I had an opportunity to test the precept some years later when I prepared to go to trial in a robbery case. The defendant, a twenty-four-year-old black man, was accused of robbing a seventy-year-old white man at gunpoint in the vestibule of a Manhattan housing project. The complainant identified the defendant from a photograph and later picked him out from a lineup containing three other people, one of whom was a police officer known to the complainant. There was no other evidence.

In preparing the case for trial, I learned that the defendant had been getting into trouble ever since he had dropped out of high school. He had been arrested several times but the charges had been dropped. He had acquired a reputation with the Housing Police who frequently picked him up for questioning. He had been convicted of a robbery two years earlier and had served six months in prison. Several days after he came home, the Housing Police picked him up again in connection with the present robbery. He had been in jail for the past fourteen months awaiting trial.

The reliability of the victim's identification was the central problem in the case. In addition to the questionable lineup, the complainant's initial description of the defendant—he told the police that his assailant was about five feet eight inches tall—differed markedly from the defendant's actual height of six feet two inches. I interviewed the complainant and questioned him closely. He was an intelligent man who gave a convincing account of the event. A jury, I thought, would probably believe him. I went to the vestibule where the crime occurred; it was well-lit, a circumstance supporting the accuracy of his identification. I talked to the janitor who had initially called the police and to several tenants. I learned nothing useful.

The defendant's lawyer protested his client's innocence, but offered no alibi. I had always found this lawyer to be professional and trustworthy. He asked, and I agreed, to have his client take a lie-detector test. He passed.

On the day before the trial, I asked the complainant to come to my office. I had spread out on my desk about twenty photographs the police officer gave me of similarly appearing males. I did not know it at the time but the spread included two photographs of the defendant. I left my office, asking the complainant to examine the photographs carefully and pick out the man who robbed him. When I returned five minutes later, he had selected a photograph of someone else; he was sure that was the person. I asked him to do it again. Again he picked out someone else. I thanked him. I explained to him that I could not prosecute the case. As I recall, he seemed to understand. My bureau chief concurred. I prepared a motion to dismiss, which the judge, expressing some reluctance, granted.

At the time, the idea that prosecutors charged individuals who were actually innocent and that juries convicted them had not yet gained national attention. Some prosecutors back then ridiculed the claim that innocent persons ever got convicted. Legendary judge Learned Hand famously called the notion that an innocent person could be convicted "an unreal dream."

Truth is elusive, and a jury's guilty verdict is not easily disproved. Today, Hand's remark appears naïve, even nonsensical. As I am writing this, the National Registry of Exonerations just reported its 2,092nd exoneree, which means an aggregate of 18,060 years of innocent persons lost in prison. Many observers believe that the number of individuals officially declared to have been wrongfully convicted is just the tip of the metaphorical iceberg.

Although the judge and a few of my colleagues were uncertain about it, and although I often reflect on it, there is no question that I did the right thing. If I allowed the case to go to trial, there is a good chance the jury would have convicted, especially if the complainant made a confident courtroom identification of the defendant. Of course, the idealized conception of the role of a prosecutor is to serve justice, convict the guilty, and free the innocent. We may assume that any responsible prosecutor standing in my shoes would have done the same thing. I hope that's right, but I'm not sure.

As I was learning how to be a responsible prosecutor, I was always conscious about what a prosecutor is supposed to do when he or she believes, or even suspects, that a defendant may be innocent. Is it the prosecutor's job to make a personal evaluation of the truth? If so, to what level of confidence must the prosecutor aspire? Or is that the jury's function only? Some of my colleagues took the "agnostic" position, arguing that even the most conscientious prosecutor could never rationally make the "extrajudicial judgment" that a seemingly reliable witness—and I am assuming that such a person is a witness with no motive to lie, as in my case above—may be unreliable. According to several of my colleagues, the prosecutor's duty is satisfied if the prosecutor alerts the court and defense counsel of the infirmities in his or her case such as questionable physical evidence or defects in a witness's credibility. I don't agree with that approach. To me, a prosecutor is a gatekeeper of justice whose most critical responsibility is to cull from the heavy volume of prosecutable cases, those cases that raise serious doubts about a defendant's guilt.

What are those cases that raise serious doubts of a defendant's guilt? I am thinking of cases that hinge on the testimony of eyewitnesses, children, police officers, and cooperating witnesses. With additional independent evidence to corroborate the testimony of these witnesses, a prosecutor's evaluation of the truth of a case is obviously strengthened, but without some other evidence, a prosecutor's reliance on the testimony of these witnesses alone is very risky. It was well-known before the advent of DNA evidence that eyewitnesses are often mistaken, confessions are sometimes false, children do fabricate, and informants are known to lie. Today, with advances in science and technology and greater scrutiny by prosecutors, the credibility of all these witnesses is more closely scrutinized.

I prosecuted several close cases and got convictions. I know in these cases there was the possibility that the defendant was innocent. There is always that risk, but careful preparation, the acquisition of corroborating evidence, a prosecutor's own intuition, and sound judgment are guideposts to making a safe and responsible decision on whether to prosecute.

Flag Desecration Cases

Several years before *Texas v. Johnson*, the Supreme Court's landmark 1984 flag-burning case, the American flag figured prominently in other criminal prosecutions. In a prominent case prosecuted by my office, a defendant named Stephen Radich, the proprietor of an art gallery on Madison Avenue, exhibited several sculptures, termed "constructions," which displayed the American flag in various provocative shapes to protest the Vietnam War. One such shape, for which he was prosecuted, depicted the American flag draped around the form of the male sexual organ, erect, and protruding upright from its base. Radich was charged under a New York statute that makes it a misdemeanor for any person to "mutilate, deface, defy, or cast contempt upon the American flag." His claim that the statute violated his right of free speech under the First Amendment was rejected.

One year after the Radich case, I was assigned my own "flag defilement" case, but my case traveled a different legal journey. With the proliferating protest demonstrations against the Vietnam War roiling the nation, my office decided to establish a special unit to prosecute these cases and I was assigned to head this unit. Most of the cases involved persons participating in protest activities who were typically charged with disorderly conduct or criminal trespass. The forms of protest varied greatly of course, from peaceful protests to violent behavior. As with the Radich case, they included conduct that disparaged the American flag.

In one case, an undercover officer went into a small bookstore on the upper west side of Manhattan and purchased a large poster depicting the American flag, but in place of the fifty stars there were fifty white doves, a symbol of peace. Inscribed over the red, white, and blue stripes were the signatures of many dozens of well-known antiwar activists. After he purchased the poster, the officer arrested the bookstore owner for violating the same New York statute under which Stephen Radich had been prosecuted.

As in *Radich*, the constitutional question was straightforward: whether the First Amendment's free speech guarantee protected the defendant from being charged and prosecuted for selling or distributing the poster. I felt it was an easier case than *Radich*. As an art form, the poster seemed more elegant, less inflammatory, and less likely to expose the flag to the kind of ridicule that the Radich sculpture provoked. I concluded that prosecuting the defendant would violate his constitutional free speech rights. I prepared my argument for dismissal.

The case was one of several hundred on the criminal court docket. The large crowded courtroom looked the same as it looks today—police officers seated in the front rows, court officers keeping the audience quiet, clerks funneling folders to the judge, correction officers escorting handcuffed defendants into and out of the courtroom. When my case was called I approached the bench, explained the background to the judge, told the judge that my office was moving to dismiss the charge, and gave as my reason our belief that the charge could not be legally sustained under the First Amendment's free speech guarantee.

The judge and I had had a relatively cordial courtroom relationship. He had a reputation for being tough but fair. He took a few moments to read the complaint, including my motion, and then denied my motion. I was startled. I didn't expect that to happen. Never in my experience did judges reject a dismissal motion by a prosecutor. (I later learned that he had recently been mugged and was not in a good mood). I explained again as calmly as I could that my office had carefully reviewed the case and decided not to prosecute it. Unmoved, the judge stared at me and repeated: "Motion denied." I felt I needed to dig in my heels as well, and so I persisted: "If Your Honor wants this case prosecuted, then Your Honor should prosecute it yourself. I won't." To this he replied loudly, "Recuse yourself from this courtroom!" I didn't know what the word "recuse" meant until Al, the court officer, whispered to me, "He wants you to get out of the courtroom."

The case was adjourned to the same part for the following month. Judges typically rotate through the parts, so there was a new judge assigned. I had never appeared before him, but I knew something about his background. He had been a deputy police commissioner before being appointed by the mayor to the criminal court. Once again I appeared for this case. When it was called I approached the bench and again asked the judge to dismiss the case. The judge was ready for me. He began by declaring, "This is a criminal charge against the defendant for desecration of the American flag.

The district attorney's motion to dismiss the charge is denied." He then, apparently from written notes, delivered a ten-minute oration on our government's commitment to freedom, democracy, and world peace, the sacrifices our nation was making to protect the American way of life, and the valor of our young soldiers who were dying on the battlefield to preserve the American flag. When the judge finished, the front two rows in the courtroom that were filled with police officers erupted in wild applause. It lasted for several minutes until the judge pretended to sternly gavel the celebration to silence.

The case was again adjourned to the following month. Now with considerable anxiety, I again entered the courtroom and asked the new judge to dismiss the case. In reflecting about this judge, the Yiddish word "mensch" comes to mind. He looked over the papers briefly, listened to my argument, and said tersely, "Case dismissed."

Needless to say, it's a case I'll never forget. I often mention it in my constitutional law class. Prosecutors often face personal conflicts and have to make difficult choices. Prosecutors are commanded to "do justice" or "do the right thing," but that's rarely a simple or easily performed command. It always depends on the individual prosecutor's sense of integrity and his or her best judgment. I suppose in the end there's a lesson here: when you believe you're doing the right thing, don't give up.

Protests and Prosecutions

During the Vietnam War, protests against the war took place throughout the nation, including in New York City. I was assigned to prosecute people arrested for participating in unlawful demonstrations and related criminal acts. I also served on a Task Force to establish police protocols during demonstrations. For whatever it's worth, the New York Civil Liberties Union wrote a nice letter to my boss about the way I handled these prosecutions.

One of the biggest demonstrations occurred at Columbia University in the spring of 1968. Students and others forcibly occupied buildings on the campus to protest two distinct university actions. First, the protesters sought to expose the university's secret affiliation with a weapons-research think-tank in the Department of Defense called the Institute for Defense Analysis. Second, the protesters sought to stop the university's construction of a new gymnasium in Morningside Park, which the protesters claimed was a segregationist effort to deny access to members of the nearby Harlem community.

In the last week of April, Columbia student activists, joined by radicals from around the country, occupied several buildings on the campus, including Low Library and Hamilton Hall, the administration building. Close to 1,000 men and women participated in these so-called "sit-ins." The demonstrators—trespassers according to the university—remained inside the buildings for several days, disregarding the university's orders to leave. The takeovers appeared to enjoy broad support from the student body and the Harlem community and gained extensive media coverage, especially from the antics of one of the leaders sitting at the university president's desk wearing sunglasses and smoking a cigar, and temporarily taking a dean hostage.

Finally, in the early morning hours of April 30, the university called in the New York City Police Department to end the demonstrations. The police stormed the buildings in riot gear using tear gas to forcibly remove the protesters from the buildings. Several police officers, students, and faculty were injured during the evacuation. More than 700 protesters were arrested.

I was assigned to prosecute the cases. I immediately decided to separate the arrests into two categories. The first group of arrests involved at least a dozen arrests for felonies involving physical violence on police officers and inciting others to physically resist arrest; these cases would receive special attention, including presentation to grand juries for indictments. The second group of cases involved the approximately 700 arrests for criminal trespass, a misdemeanor, based on the complaint of the property owner, the university.

As I prepared the trespass cases I quickly recognized a serious problem of proof. I interviewed the police officers involved in the removal and arrests. The officers were completely candid about the planning and execution of the operation. The protocol, as I learned, involved police officers in riot gear entering the buildings, physically detaining the individuals inside, and then forcibly removing them from the buildings. The problem was that the officers who entered the buildings and removed the students were not the ones who then took custody of the persons arrested, directed them onto buses, and carted them off for booking and arraignment downtown. No photos were taken of any of the protesters to show where they were situated when they were physically removed and locked up. In other words, I questioned whether I could prove under a charge of criminal trespass that a person arrested and booked was the same person who was physically present inside the building. I concluded that the cases could not be successfully prosecuted with any realistic hope of a getting a conviction.

While I was deliberating whether I could successfully prosecute these cases from a factual proof standpoint, the university was also undertaking its own prosecution analysis, not from a proof standpoint but from a very different perspective—the damage to its reputation from the protests and future litigation. The university had already disaffiliated itself from the Institute for Defense Analysis and scrapped its plans for the gymnasium. A group of administrators, faculty, and students was formed to advise the Board of Trustees on appropriate discipline for the students involved, including criminal prosecution for trespass. After considerable discussion, the university decided to withdraw its trespass complaint against the protesters. The university wished to close the book on the case, at least insofar as criminal prosecution of the trespassers was concerned. I took this as quite a relief. Since prosecuting the cases would be factually impossible anyway, having to request the dismissal of 700 cases based on factual insufficiency would be embarrassing both to the police department and the district attorney. Dismissal based on the university's action was a much better outcome.

The cases were placed on the court calendar. Several distinguished attorneys represented the defendants pro bono—legal work undertaken without charge. They had been involved in several discussions with the university culminating in the university's agreement to withdraw the charges of trespass. With this concession, the lawyers prepared motions to dismiss, but there was a catch, and a very big one. A prosecutor does not represent a private party; a prosecutor represents the public. The prosecutor's task is to serve justice as the prosecutor sees it. So, the university's decision to withdraw its complaint, while compelling, does not necessarily foreclose a prosecutor from rejecting that concession if the prosecutor believes that the public interest demands prosecution.

These were my cases and I had to answer the defendants' motions. These were important cases. We were on the spot. I strongly believed it would be the right thing for my office not to oppose the motions, both because of the practical difficulty of convicting, and to at least show deference to the university's willingness to end the ordeal of prosecution and begin to heal the discord.

I explained my views to the district attorney. We talked for a long time. He listened carefully to my position but he disagreed with me. He wanted me to oppose the motions to dismiss. I tried to convince him that regardless of the university's position, I probably would not be able to prosecute these cases anyway. His response was upsetting and disappointing. I really didn't know what to do. Whether or not his decision was influenced by the fact that he was a prominent member of Columbia's Board of Trustees and an active supporter of the university, I do not know. I finally told him that I could not go into court and oppose the motions to dismiss. I think the district attorney understood, at least I want to think he did. We agreed that my bureau chief would appear in court to oppose the university's motion.

On the day scheduled for the motions to be argued, my bureau chief spoke, without much enthusiasm as I recall. His argument repeated the formalistic arguments that prosecutors typically make: the protesters willfully violated the law, the law needed to be vindicated, and lawbreakers needed to be punished. The lawyers for the defendants argued that there really was no serious public harm, the private party was willing to forego criminal prosecution for the harm it may have suffered, and the defendants were contrite about what they did. Nothing was said about the fact that if the judge denied the motions and directed the cases to proceed to trial, the prosecution could not in good faith proceed to trial with any hope of obtaining a conviction.

The judge declared a short recess.

Fifteen minutes later he returned with his decision. Motions granted, cases dismissed.

My colleagues needled me; I had lost more cases in one day than any prosecutor had lost in an entire career.